FINDING YOURSELF

FINDING YOURSELF

COURTNEY THOMAS

CONTENTS

CHAPTER 1

The Overwhelmed Woman

The Modern Woman's Juggling Act:
The modern woman is a symphony of roles. She's the nurturing mother, the devoted wife, the ambitious employee, the dutiful daughter, the loyal friend, and often, she tries to be all of these things simultaneously. We wear countless hats, juggling responsibilities with a smile, a determined spirit, and a constant, low-grade hum of anxiety that whispers, "You're not doing enough." This is the modern woman's juggling act – a performance that requires constant attention, superhuman multitasking skills, and a relentless determination to keep all the balls in the air.

We are conditioned to believe that we can, and must, do it all. This expectation stems from a societal narrative that glorifies the "superwoman" archetype, a mythical creature who effortlessly manages career ambitions, pristine homes, and happy families, all while maintaining a flawless appearance. The reality is far from this idealized image. The pressure to be everything to everyone is immense. We are expected to be successful in our careers, raise well-adjusted children, maintain a thriving social life, keep a spotless home, and still find time for self-care. It's a relentless barrage of expectations, and the weight of it can be crushing.

The reality is that we are not superwomen. We are human beings with limitations, and trying to live up to these impossible standards only leads to burnout, resentment, and a sense of inadequacy. Think about your own life. How many roles do you juggle? Do you feel overwhelmed by the demands placed on you? Is there a constant tension between what you *should* be doing and what you *want* to do? The feeling of being overwhelmed is not a sign of weakness. It's a sign that you are a human being, capable of feeling and experiencing the world around you. It's a sign that you are trying to do too much and that you need to make some changes.

Imagine a woman named Sarah. Sarah is a successful lawyer, a loving wife, and a dedicated mother of two young children. She wakes up at 5 am every day to get a head start on her work, then rushes to get her children ready for school before heading to the office. She works long hours, often sacrificing her lunch break to catch up on emails. After work, she picks up her children, attends their soccer games, and prepares dinner. She finally gets a few moments to herself in the evening before falling asleep, exhausted but feeling a nagging sense of guilt for not spending more time with her family.

This is a familiar story for many women. We feel an immense pressure to excel in every aspect of our lives, striving for a level of perfection that is both unattainable and ultimately unsustainable. We are constantly comparing ourselves to others, scrolling through social media feeds filled with curated highlights of "perfect" lives. This relentless comparison is a recipe for self-doubt and unhappiness. It makes us feel inadequate, as if we are always falling short of some imagined ideal.

However, this narrative is flawed. The "perfect" life portrayed on social media is often a carefully constructed illusion, a facade carefully crafted to hide the struggles and imperfections of real life. It's time to stop buying into this unrealistic standard. It's time to acknowledge the reality of our lives, with all their messy imperfections, and give ourselves permission to be human. This is not about lowering our standards; it's about shifting our perspective. It's about recognizing that being "perfect" is not the goal; it's about finding balance, prioritizing what matters most, and embracing the unique beauty of our own journey.

There are many ways to find balance and reclaim your sense of self amidst the chaos. It's about finding ways to say "no" to things that don't serve you, setting boundaries, and prioritizing your own well-being. The modern woman's juggling act is not about being everything to everyone; it's about being authentically ourselves. It's about finding our own rhythm and creating a life that feels fulfilling and sustainable. But first, we need to acknowledge the pressure we feel, the exhaustion we carry, and the sense of inadequacy that often weighs us down. We need to acknowledge that we are not alone in this struggle, and that there is nothing wrong with feeling overwhelmed. It's time to give ourselves permission to breathe. It's time to accept the struggle and embrace our humanity. It's time to find our self-worth in the midst of it all.

This is a journey of self-discovery and empowerment. It's a journey of finding our voice, setting our own boundaries, and creating a life that reflects our true values and priorities. This journey starts with recognizing the signs of being overwhelmed, accepting the struggle, and learning to prioritize ourselves without guilt or shame. This is the foundation upon which we will build a life of balance, fulfillment, and true self-worth.

The Price of Perfection:

The pressure to be perfect is a constant companion for many women. It's woven into the fabric of our society, whispered through countless media messages, and reinforced by the expectations of those around us. We're bombarded with images of flawless beauty, effortless success, and the seemingly seamless juggling of multiple demanding roles. From a young age, we're taught that a "good girl" is obedient, helpful, and always striving for perfection. This pressure to achieve the impossible can lead to a crippling sense of inadequacy and self-doubt.

We internalize these messages, believing that our worth is tied to our ability to meet these unrealistic standards. We strive to be the perfect wife, the perfect mother, the perfect employee, the perfect friend, all while maintaining a perfectly sculpted body and a perfectly organized home. The weight of these expectations can be overwhelming, pushing us to the brink of exhaustion and leaving us feeling like we're constantly failing to measure up. Think about it: how many times have you felt the sting of societal expectations? Perhaps you've been criticized for not being a "good enough" mother because you work outside the home, or for not being a "good enough" wife because you prioritize your career. Maybe you've been made to feel inadequate because you haven't achieved the "ideal" body shape, or because your house doesn't look like it's been professionally staged.

These expectations aren't just confined to our personal lives. The workplace, too, can be a pressure cooker of expectations. Women often face the double standard of needing to be assertive but not "too aggressive," of proving their competence but not "threatening" male colleagues. The subtle, and sometimes overt, messaging around our appearance, our demeanor, and our achievements can create a constant undercurrent of anxiety and pressure. It's important to acknowledge that these expectations are often rooted in outdated societal norms and stereotypes. We are constantly bombarded with messages that perpetuate the notion of women being subservient, nurturing, and primarily focused on domestic life. These messages are deeply ingrained in our culture, and they can be difficult to shake off.

But here's the truth: these expectations are simply not realistic. They are designed to make us feel inadequate, to keep us striving for an unattainable ideal. They are designed to silence our voices, to limit our ambitions, and to keep us from fully realizing our potential. We must remember that we are not obligated to conform to these expectations. We are not required to live up to an impossible standard of perfection. We are allowed to have flaws, to make mistakes, and to prioritize our own well-being. We are allowed to say "no," to set boundaries, and to redefine success on our own terms. It's time to break free from the tyranny of perfection. It's time to reclaim our power and embrace our authentic selves. We deserve to live lives that are free from the pressure to conform, free from the burden of unrealistic expectations. We deserve to live lives that are true to ourselves, that are filled with joy, purpose, and fulfillment.

The journey of self-worth begins with the realization that perfection is a myth. It's a mirage, a constantly shifting target that we will never reach. Instead of chasing this elusive ideal, we must embrace our imperfections, our flaws, and our unique strengths. It's in these imperfections that we find our true beauty, our true power, and our true worth. It's also important to recognize that the pressure to be perfect is often fueled by fear. We fear that if we don't meet these expectations, we won't be loved, accepted, or valued. We fear that we won't be good enough. But this fear is a false prophet. Our worth is not determined by our ability to achieve perfection. It's inherent, it's intrinsic, it's ours from the moment we are born. So, let's start to dismantle the myth of perfection. Let's challenge these unrealistic expectations. Let's embrace our imperfections, our flaws, and our unique strengths. Let's live our lives authentically, with confidence and purpose. We are enough, just as we are. And that is a truth worth celebrating.

The path to self-worth requires that we become aware of the societal pressures we face. It's not about blaming society, but about acknowledging the insidious messages that can chip away at our confidence. By becoming aware of these pressures, we can start to challenge them, to question them, and to ultimately resist their influence. We can start by questioning the media we consume. Are we being bombarded with images of unrealistic beauty standards? Are we being fed messages that suggest our worth is tied to our appearance, our accomplishments, or our possessions? If so, it's time to step back and reconsider the messages we're absorbing. We can also challenge the expectations of those around us. Are we being pressured to live up to a certain standard of behavior, appearance, or achievement? If so, it's time to set boundaries, to communicate our needs, and to prioritize our own well-being. We are not obligated to meet these expectations, and we have the power to say "no."

Finally, we can challenge the expectations we place on ourselves. Are we constantly striving for perfection, for an unrealistic ideal? Are we punishing ourselves for our mistakes and shortcomings? If so, it's time to practice self-compassion, to embrace our imperfections, and to celebrate our successes. By challenging the pressure to be perfect, we can create a more authentic, more fulfilling, and more empowered life. We can break free from the shackles of unrealistic expectations and embrace the freedom of being ourselves. It's a journey, not a destination. It's a process of constant self-discovery and evolution. But it's a journey worth taking, a journey that can lead us to a life that is true to ourselves, a life that is filled with purpose, and a life that is overflowing with self-worth.

Here are some additional points to consider: The impact of social media: The relentless stream of curated and often unrealistic images on social media platforms can exacerbate feelings of inadequacy and self-doubt. It's important to be mindful of our social media consumption and to curate our feeds to include content that is positive, inspiring, and supportive. We can also choose to follow accounts that promote body positivity, self-acceptance, and a more realistic view of life.

The pressure to be a "supermom": The expectation that women should be able to "do it all" without showing any signs of stress or fatigue is unrealistic and harmful. The pressure to be a "supermom" can lead to feelings of guilt, shame, and exhaustion. It's important to acknowledge that we can't be everything to everyone, and to prioritize our own well-being. We can also seek support from our partners, family, and friends, and recognize that asking for help is not a sign of weakness but a sign of strength.

The beauty industry: The beauty industry is a multi-billion-dollar industry built on the notion that women need to buy products to fix their "flaws." This messaging can be incredibly damaging, leading women to feel insecure about their appearance and to spend exorbitant amounts of money on products that promise to make them look perfect. It's important to challenge these messages, to embrace our natural beauty, and to recognize that true beauty comes from within.

The impact of cultural norms: Cultural norms play a significant role in shaping our expectations of what it means to be a woman. It's important to be aware of these norms and to question whether they are truly serving us. We can also seek out role models who are challenging these norms, who are embracing their authenticity, and who are showing us that it's possible to live a life that is true to ourselves.

The Warning Signs:

The overwhelming feeling, a familiar sensation that has become a constant companion for many women, is often accompanied by a cascade of physical, emotional, and mental symptoms. It's like a silent alarm, signaling that the body and mind are struggling to keep up with the demands of life. Recognizing these warning signs is the first step towards understanding the depth of the struggle and taking action to reclaim your well-being.

Physical Signs: The most immediate and noticeable signs of overwhelm often manifest physically. Fatigue, a constant companion to the overwhelmed woman, can range from mild tiredness to debilitating exhaustion. Sleep becomes elusive, with insomnia or frequent awakenings disrupting restful nights. The body feels heavy, as if carrying an invisible weight, making even simple tasks seem daunting. Headaches, muscle tension, and digestive issues may become frequent occurrences, adding to the growing sense of unease.

Emotional Signs: The emotional landscape of overwhelm is equally turbulent. Anxiety, a persistent feeling of unease and dread, can linger in the background or surge into full-blown panic. Irritability becomes a dominant emotion, making it difficult to remain patient or calm, particularly in challenging situations. Fear, a nagging sense of vulnerability and inadequacy, can cloud judgment and create self-doubt. Feeling overwhelmed can lead to a sense of isolation and disconnection, creating a longing for support and understanding.

Mental Signs: The mental toll of overwhelm is equally significant. Difficulty concentrating, a common symptom, makes it challenging to focus on tasks, leading to missed deadlines and errors in judgment.

Decision-making becomes a daunting process, as simple choices seem overwhelming and fraught with potential consequences. Overthinking, a relentless cycle of negative thoughts and worries, consumes mental energy and hinders problem-solving. Memory lapses and forgetfulness become more frequent, adding to the frustration and sense of being overwhelmed.

Understanding the Connection: These physical, emotional, and mental symptoms are interconnected, forming a complex cycle of stress and exhaustion. Physical fatigue can exacerbate anxiety and contribute to difficulty concentrating, while emotional distress can manifest in physical symptoms like headaches or digestive problems. The mental exhaustion caused by overwhelm can further amplify emotional distress and lead to feelings of hopelessness and despair.

The Importance of Recognizing the Signs: Ignoring these warning signs only fuels the cycle of overwhelm. It is crucial to acknowledge these changes in your body and mind as signals that you need to prioritize your well-being. Recognizing these signs allows you to take proactive steps to manage your stress, address the underlying causes of overwhelm, and begin the journey towards a more balanced and fulfilling life.

Self-Compassion and Acceptance: Recognizing the signs of overwhelm can be a challenging but necessary step. It requires honesty, self-awareness, and a willingness to acknowledge that you are not alone in this struggle. Many women experience these symptoms, and recognizing them is a sign of strength, not weakness. Instead of judging yourself or feeling ashamed, embrace self-compassion and acceptance. Allow yourself to acknowledge the struggle and understand that you are not failing; you are simply experiencing the natural consequences of pushing yourself too far.

Embracing Imperfection: Perfectionism, a societal expectation often internalized by women, can contribute to feelings of overwhelm. The relentless pursuit of perfection creates unrealistic expectations and a constant sense of inadequacy. Embrace imperfection and understand that it is okay to make mistakes, to have off days, and to prioritize your well-being without guilt or shame.

The Power of Small Steps: The journey out of overwhelm is not a quick fix. It requires patience, self-compassion, and a willingness to take small steps towards change. Start by addressing one symptom at a time, whether it's getting more sleep, practicing mindfulness techniques to manage anxiety, or simplifying your daily routine. Remember, every small step you take towards prioritizing your well-being is a step in the right direction.

Building a Support System: Seeking support from loved ones, friends, or a therapist can be invaluable in navigating the challenges of overwhelm. Sharing your experiences with someone who understands and cares can provide a sense of validation and offer practical advice. A therapist can provide a safe space to explore the roots of overwhelm, develop coping mechanisms, and build a plan for creating a more balanced life.

The Path to Empowerment: Recognizing the signs of overwhelm is the first step on a journey towards empowerment. By acknowledging the struggle, practicing self-compassion, and taking small steps towards change, you can reclaim your well-being and break free from the cycle of overwhelm. Remember, you are worthy of a life filled with balance, joy, and fulfillment. Embrace the journey, celebrate your strength, and trust in your ability to create the life you deserve.

Permission To Breathe:

It's time to acknowledge the elephant in the room, the one we've been tiptoeing around, ignoring, and pretending doesn't exist. It's okay to admit it. We're overwhelmed. And it's not a sign of weakness; it's a sign of the strength we've been carrying, the weight of expectations, the relentless demands of our lives, and the societal pressure to be everything to everyone. But here's the thing, my dear reader: you are not alone. We all have our struggles, our anxieties, our moments where we feel like we're drowning in a sea of "to-dos" and "should-dos."

Imagine this: you're juggling a thousand balls in the air—work deadlines, school events, family obligations, personal goals, and the constant need to be present and perfect. It's a breathtaking act, a spectacle of multi-tasking and superhuman endurance. But deep down, you're feeling the strain. The pressure to maintain this relentless juggling act is taking its toll. The whispers start to creep in: "You should be doing more," "You're not doing enough," "You need to be a better wife, a better mother, a better employee." The pressure builds, and you feel the weight of those expectations tightening around your chest. But here's the truth: the "shoulds" are a mirage, a smoke screen created by societal pressures and unrealistic expectations. They're not real. They're a collective narrative we've been fed, a story that we've internalized, and it's time to rewrite the script.

The first step is to give yourself permission to breathe. To acknowledge the struggle, the fatigue, the overwhelm. And to say, "It's okay. It's okay to not be okay." It's okay to feel the weight, the pressure, the exhaustion. It's not a sign of weakness, but a sign of resilience, of the strength you've been carrying. You are not a machine. You are a human being, a complex and multifaceted individual with needs, wants, and limitations. And it's okay to admit that you have limits, that you can't be everything to everyone, that you can't do it all. Imagine yourself standing on the shore of a vast ocean, the waves crashing against the sand. The ocean represents the overwhelming demands of life, the constant flow of expectations, the pressure to perform. And you, standing on the shore, are the one trying to control the waves, to manage their power, to keep them at bay. But the truth is, you can't control the ocean. You can't control the waves. You can only learn to ride them, to navigate their currents, to find your own rhythm and flow.

This is where self-compassion comes in. It's about acknowledging your own humanity, your own vulnerabilities, and treating yourself with the same kindness and understanding you would extend to a loved one in need. When you're feeling overwhelmed, exhausted, or on the verge of burnout, don't judge yourself. Don't criticize or berate yourself. Instead, offer yourself a warm embrace, a gentle hand on your shoulder, a whispered word of encouragement. Tell yourself, "It's okay. I'm doing my best." "I am strong. I am capable. I am worthy of love and care."

Self-compassion isn't about giving up or giving in. It's about recognizing your limitations, honoring your needs, and finding ways to navigate the challenges of life with grace and resilience. It's about understanding that you are worthy of love, care, and compassion, even when you make mistakes, fall short of expectations, or feel overwhelmed. It's about giving yourself permission to breathe. To prioritize your well-being. To listen to your inner voice. To create space for self-care. Imagine a quiet room, bathed in soft light. You're sitting in a comfortable chair, a cup of warm tea in your hands. You close your eyes, and take a deep, slow breath. The air fills your lungs, and you feel a sense of calm wash over you. You're not running, you're not rushing, you're not trying to control the world. You're simply breathing, allowing yourself to be present in this moment.

This is the power of self-compassion. It's about creating that space, that sanctuary, that moment of peace within yourself, even amidst the chaos and demands of daily life. Remember: you are not alone. We all struggle with overwhelm. We all have those moments where we feel like we're drowning in the sea of "should-dos." But you're not broken. You're not weak. You're simply human. And you're worthy of compassion, care, and love. Give yourself permission to breathe. And remember, it's okay to not be okay. This is your journey, your story. And you have the power to write the ending you desire. So, take a deep breath, and step into the light of self-compassion. You are strong. You are worthy. You are capable. You are loved.

The Power of Perspective:
The shift from "should" to "want" is a subtle yet powerful transformation that can significantly impact how you navigate your life. It's about moving away from the relentless pressure to fulfill societal expectations and embracing the freedom to prioritize what truly matters

to you. Imagine a woman who feels obligated to be the perfect wife, mother, and employee. She wakes up early, prepares breakfast for her family, rushes to work, tackles a demanding workload, picks up the kids from school, makes dinner, and finally collapses onto the couch, exhausted. She's fulfilling all the "shoulds" – she should be a loving wife, a nurturing mother, a dedicated worker – but she's losing sight of her own needs and desires.

This constant pressure to conform to societal expectations can be incredibly draining. It can lead to feelings of guilt, resentment, and inadequacy. But what if she shifted her perspective? What if she stopped focusing on what she "should" be doing and started exploring what she genuinely "wants" from life? Maybe she wants to spend more time pursuing her passion for painting. Maybe she wants to prioritize her physical and mental well-being by taking a yoga class or meditating each morning. Maybe she wants to travel the world and experience different cultures. Shifting from "should" to "want" doesn't mean abandoning her responsibilities or neglecting her loved ones. It's about finding a balance – a balance that allows her to fulfill her obligations while also prioritizing her own well-being and pursuing her passions.

Here are some practical steps you can take to cultivate this shift in your own life: Become aware of your "shoulds": Pay close attention to the thoughts that pop into your head that begin with "I should..." These are often rooted in societal expectations, not your own desires Question those "shoulds": Once you've identified those "shoulds," challenge them. Ask yourself: "Is this really what I want, or is it something I feel pressured to do?" Listen to your inner voice: Pay attention to your own needs, desires, and dreams. What are you truly passionate about? What makes you feel fulfilled? Prioritize your "wants": Make a conscious effort to schedule time for activities that bring you joy and fulfillment. These could be hobbies, personal projects, time spent with loved ones, or simply moments of quiet reflection. Be kind to yourself: This journey of prioritizing your "wants" might be challenging but be patient and compassionate with yourself. It takes time to break free from ingrained patterns of behavior and societal conditioning.

Remember, your life is your own. You have the power to choose how you spend your time, energy, and resources. You don't need to live by someone else's expectations. Embrace the freedom to define what truly matters to you and prioritize your "wants" over the "shoulds." This shift in perspective can be a transformative experience. It can help you rediscover your passion, reclaim your sense of self, and create a life that is both fulfilling and meaningful. Let's delve into some real-life examples to illustrate how this shift can manifest in everyday life:

Example 1: The Busy Mom

Meet Sarah, a mother of two young children, a full-time job, and a busy social life. She juggles work, home responsibilities, and social obligations, feeling perpetually overwhelmed and exhausted. Her days are filled with "shoulds": she should be a present and attentive mother, she should be a supportive wife, she should excel at her job, she should be a good friend, and she should host a dinner party for her husband's colleagues. The list goes on. But Sarah feels like she's constantly running on empty. She rarely has time for herself, and she's starting to feel resentful of all the "shoulds" that are dictating her life. She's longing for something more – a sense of fulfillment beyond her daily obligations.

One day, she decides to shift her perspective. She takes a moment to reflect on what she truly "wants." She realizes that she wants to spend more time with her children, but not just by rushing them through a schedule of activities. She wants to be present, engaged, and truly enjoys their company. She also wants to rediscover her love for painting, a passion she'd put on hold when her children were born. Sarah makes a conscious decision to prioritize her "wants." She starts by carving out just 30 minutes each day to paint, even if it means waking up a little earlier. She also starts saying "no" to some social commitments that drain her energy. The shift from "should" to "want" might seem small, but it creates a ripple effect in her life. Sarah feels more energized, more connected to her children, and more fulfilled in her creative pursuits. She's still a busy mom, but she's no longer solely defined by her responsibilities. She's rediscovering her identity and prioritizing what truly matters to her.

Example 2: The Career Woman

Meet Emily, a successful lawyer who feels perpetually stuck in a cycle of work and obligation. She's constantly striving for perfection in her career, sacrificing personal time and relationships to climb the corporate ladder. She's fulfilling all the "shoulds" – she should be a high-achieving lawyer, she should be a strong and independent woman, she should be at the top of her game. But Emily is starting to feel a sense of emptiness. She's missing out on experiences and connections that enrich her life. She wants to travel, learn new skills, and connect with her friends on a deeper level. She's longing for a life that extends beyond her professional achievements. Emily decides to shift her perspective. She takes a step back and asks herself: "What do I truly want from life?" She realizes that she wants to pursue her passion for photography. She also wants to spend more time with her family and friends. She wants to create a life that is not just successful but also fulfilling and balanced. Emily starts making changes. She schedules a photography class, she sets aside time to connect with loved ones, and she starts saying "no" to projects that don't align with her goals. The shift from "should" to "want" brings Emily a sense of peace and clarity. She's still driven and ambitious, but she's no longer sacrificing her well-being and happiness for the sake of her career. She's embracing a more balanced and fulfilling life, one that aligns with her values and passions.

Example 3: The Overwhelmed Wife

Meet Jessica, a wife who feels constantly pressured to be the perfect homemaker and caretaker. She's responsible for cooking, cleaning, managing the household finances, and keeping everything running smoothly. She also feels a sense of obligation to attend every social event and always be available for her husband's family. Jessica's days are filled with "shoulds": she should be an excellent cook, she should keep the house spotless, she should be a gracious hostess, she should be a supportive and understanding wife, and she should be available for her husband's every need. But Jessica is starting to feel overwhelmed and resentful. She's constantly exhausted and she's losing sight of her own needs. She wants to pursue her love for writing, she wants to spend time on personal hobbies, and she wants to have more time to relax and recharge. Jessica decides to shift her perspective. She asks herself: "What do I truly want from my marriage?" She realizes that she wants to have an equal partnership, where both she and her husband share responsibilities and contribute equally to the household. She also wants to cultivate a relationship that is based on mutual respect, open communication, and shared interests. Jessica starts having honest conversations with her husband. She expresses her feelings and she asks for his support in sharing responsibilities. She also sets clear boundaries around her time and energy. The shift from "should" to "want" leads to a more equitable and fulfilling marriage for Jessica. She's no longer the sole caretaker or homemaker. She's sharing responsibilities with her husband, and she's creating space for her own needs and passions.

Beyond the examples:

These examples highlight how shifting from "should" to "want" can be a powerful catalyst for change. It's not about abandoning your responsibilities or neglecting your loved ones. It's about finding a balance that honors your own needs and desires, while also allowing you to contribute to the relationships and commitments that are important to you. This shift in perspective can be a journey of self-discovery. It's about listening to your inner voice, uncovering your passions, and setting intentions that align with what truly matters to you. It's about reclaiming your identity and creating a life that is both meaningful and fulfilling.

A final note: The shift from "should" to "want" is not always easy. It might involve challenging ingrained patterns of behavior, pushing back against societal expectations, and having difficult conversations with loved ones. But it's worth it. It's worth it for the sense of freedom, fulfillment, and self-worth that comes with prioritizing what genuinely matters to you. So, take a moment to reflect on your own life. What are the "shoulds" that are dictating your actions and your choices? What are the "wants" that are buried beneath the surface, longing for attention and expression? And then, take a step towards embracing those "wants." You deserve a life that is filled with joy, passion, and purpose. You deserve to live a life that is truly your own.

CHAPTER 2

Reclaiming Your Identity

Beyond The Roles:
It's easy to get caught up in the whirlwind of daily life, especially as women. We navigate the delicate dance of motherhood, the complexities of marriage, the demands of work, and the constant pull of societal expectations. We wear many hats, and often, our own identities get lost in the shuffle. It's a common experience to wake up one morning and realize, "Who am I beyond these roles?" The journey to reclaiming your identity starts with a simple question: who are you beyond the responsibilities that define your days? Think about it – who are you beyond being a mother, wife, employee, daughter, sister, friend? These roles are important, undoubtedly, but they don't define your essence. Beneath these roles lies a unique and vibrant individual, a woman with her own dreams, aspirations, and passions. It's time to reconnect with that woman, the woman you are beyond the labels.

This journey of self-discovery might seem daunting at first. You may be thinking, "I barely have time to breathe, how can I possibly uncover a hidden part of myself?" But this is where the magic happens. It doesn't have to be an elaborate process. Start small, with simple moments of reflection. Imagine yourself on a quiet morning, sipping your coffee, before the day's chaos begins. Take a moment to breathe, to feel the warmth of the sun on your skin, and to simply be present with yourself. In these moments of quiet contemplation, ask yourself questions that delve beneath the surface. What brings you joy? What makes your heart sing? What are you passionate about? It could be anything – painting, writing, dancing, gardening, traveling, reading, or simply spending time in nature. It doesn't matter what it is, as long as it sparks something within you.

Perhaps you used to have hobbies that got pushed aside due to the demands of life. Remember those passions – the ones that brought you a sense of fulfillment and excitement. Think about those forgotten interests – the art supplies gathering dust in the attic, the travel magazines tucked away in a drawer, the musical instrument collecting cobwebs in the corner. These are fragments of your authentic self, waiting to be rekindled.

There's a powerful energy that flows from embracing your passions. It's a spark that ignites a sense of purpose and fulfillment, even amidst the everyday chaos. It reminds you that you are more than just a collection of roles. You are a woman with a unique set of talents, desires, and dreams. This journey of self-discovery is not about abandoning your roles or neglecting your responsibilities. It's about finding a balance – a harmony between your commitments and your personal growth. It's about understanding that you can be a loving mother, a devoted wife, a dedicated employee, and still carve out space for your own passions and interests. It's a delicate balancing act, a constant dance between giving and receiving, between fulfilling your obligations and pursuing your own aspirations. It's about recognizing that you have a right to nurture your own well-being without feeling guilty or selfish.

Imagine a life where you can embrace all the facets of your being without sacrificing your identity. Imagine a life where you can wear the hat of a mother, a wife, an employee, and still be the vibrant, passionate woman you were born to be. This is not a utopia; it's a journey, a gradual process of reclaiming your identity, one step at a time. Start by carving out small pockets of time for yourself. It could be 15 minutes in the morning to read a book, 30 minutes in the evening to write in a journal, or an hour on the weekend to pursue a hobby. Find small ways to nourish your soul, to reconnect with the woman who lies beneath the surface. As you explore your interests, you may discover hidden talents or long-forgotten dreams. Embrace these discoveries with enthusiasm. It's never too late to explore a new passion, to pick up a paintbrush, to take a dance class, to learn a new language, or to travel to a far-off land. These experiences will not only enrich your life but also help you rediscover the woman you truly are.

There will be moments when you feel overwhelmed, when you feel pulled in a thousand directions. It's okay to feel this way. It's part of the human experience. But remember to pause, to take a deep breath, and to remind yourself that you have the power to choose. You have the power to carve out time for yourself, to prioritize your needs, and to pursue your dreams. This journey of self-discovery is a lifelong process, a continuous unfolding of your authentic self. It's about embracing the complexities of life while honoring the woman you are at your core. So, take a deep breath, trust your instincts, and embark on this journey of rediscovery. The woman you are waiting to be found, and she's more extraordinary than you can imagine.

Uncovering Your Values:

Imagine you're holding a treasure map, its faded lines pointing to a buried chest filled with jewels. This map isn't one you find in a dusty attic; it's a map to your own inner world, a journey of self-discovery leading to the heart of your values. These values, like the jewels in the treasure chest, are the guiding stars that illuminate your path, shaping your choices, and defining the life you truly want to live. But how do you find these hidden gems? How do you decipher the whispers of your soul amidst the clamor of daily life? It starts with a simple question: What matters most to you? This isn't about the things you *think* you should value, or the ideals you've absorbed from society, family, or friends. This is about delving into the core of your being, identifying the principles that truly resonate with your soul.

Think of it as peeling back the layers of an onion. You start with the outer layers, the superficial desires and expectations – a nice house, a successful career, a picture-perfect family. But as you peel back these layers, you uncover a deeper truth, a set of values that are fundamental to your happiness and well-being. Here's a practical approach to uncovering your values: Reflect on Your Past: Recall moments that made you feel truly alive, where you experienced a sense of fulfillment or deep satisfaction. What were you doing? What values did those experiences reflect? For example, if you remember a time you felt deeply connected to nature, your values might include connection, peace, and appreciation for beauty.

Consider Your Inspirations: Who are the people you admire? What qualities do you respect most in them? Their actions often reflect their values, providing insight into your own. Examine Your Reactions: Pay attention to the situations that make you feel happy, sad, angry, or frustrated. These emotions can be powerful indicators of what you value. For instance, if you feel angry when someone betrays your trust, it might be a sign that you value honesty and integrity. Explore Your Dreams: What are your aspirations? What do you long to achieve in life? These aspirations often point to the values that drive your goals. If you dream of starting your own business, you likely value independence, creativity, and self-reliance. Journal Your Insights: As you explore these questions, write down your thoughts and feelings in a journal. This act of reflection helps solidify your understanding and allows you to revisit your insights as you continue your journey.

Remember: Values Are Unique: Your values are as unique as your fingerprint, shaped by your experiences, personality, and life journey. There's no right or wrong answer, no universal list that applies to everyone. Values Can Evolve: Your values can change over time as you grow and learn. Embrace this evolution as a sign of personal growth and a reflection of your evolving understanding of yourself. Values Are Your Compass: Once you uncover your values, they become your compass, guiding your decisions and actions. They empower you to say "yes" to opportunities that align with your core beliefs and say "no" to those that don't.

The Value of Defining Your Values

Knowing your values is more than just an intellectual exercise; it's a transformative process that unlocks your potential and empowers you to live a more fulfilling life. Here's how understanding your values can benefit you: Clarity and Purpose: Values provide a clear framework for making decisions, setting priorities, and pursuing your goals. They create a sense of purpose and direction, guiding you toward a life that aligns with your deepest beliefs. Enhanced Self-Awareness: By identifying your core values, you gain a deeper understanding of yourself, your strengths, and your limitations. This self-awareness allows you to make choices that are aligned with your true nature. Improved Relationships: Understanding your own values helps you better understand the values of others. This empathy and respect create stronger connections and more fulfilling relationships. Greater Resilience: When you are anchored in your values, you become more resilient in the face of challenges. You are less likely to be swayed by external pressures and more likely to stand firm in your beliefs. Increased Happiness: Living in alignment with your values brings a sense of peace, contentment, and overall well-being. It allows you to focus on what truly matters, creating a life filled with meaning and purpose.

Remember: This is just the beginning of your journey. Uncovering your values is a continuous process of exploration and self-discovery. Be patient with yourself, embrace the journey, and allow your values to guide you toward a life that reflects your true self.

Igniting Your Passions

This is a time for introspection, for unearthing the hidden treasures of your soul and reigniting the flames of passion that may have been dormant for years. We all have inherent talents and interests, some nurtured from childhood, others waiting to be discovered. These passions, like flickering embers, hold the potential to illuminate our lives with joy, purpose, and a renewed sense of self. Imagine a child, captivated by the vibrant colors of a paintbrush, swirling them across a canvas, unburdened by self-doubt, and lost in the creative flow. This is the essence of passion — a pure, unadulterated joy in the act of doing. As we grow older, however, the demands of life, the pressure to conform, and the weight of responsibilities can sometimes overshadow these innate desires. But just as a seed buried deep beneath the earth can sprout into a magnificent tree, so too can our passions be rekindled, given the right nurturing.

Remember that time you spent hours engrossed in a book, completely absorbed in another world, or the joy of baking that perfect batch of cookies, the aroma filling your home with warmth and comfort. These are the whispers of your passions, waiting to be heard. They are the sparks that ignite a sense of purpose, adding depth and meaning to our lives. The journey of reclaiming our passions begins with a simple question: What brought you joy in the past? Perhaps it was the thrill of writing, the satisfaction of creating something with your hands, the rhythm of music, the quiet solitude of nature, or the joy of connecting with others through meaningful conversations. These are not just hobbies; they are reflections of your authentic self, waiting to be embraced once more.

Don't be afraid to delve into the past, to explore the corners of your memory where forgotten dreams and aspirations reside. Ask yourself: What activities did you find yourself drawn to as a child? What did you spend your free time doing? What hobbies did you neglect as life got busier? Allow yourself to daydream, to lose yourself in the possibilities. What if you were to pick up that paintbrush again, or enroll in that pottery class you've always wanted to try? What if you were to rediscover the joy of playing music or writing a poem? The key is to approach this exploration with a sense of curiosity and openness, free from judgment. Don't get caught up in the "shoulds" and "shouldn't" of society, or the fear of failure. This is about rediscovering your own unique rhythm, your personal symphony of passions.

But this journey isn't just about revisiting the past. It's also about embracing the unknown, about venturing into the uncharted territories of your interests. There's a world of possibilities waiting to be explored, from the art of calligraphy to the science of astronomy, from the magic of photography to the thrill of hiking in the wilderness. Don't be afraid to try something new, to step outside your comfort zone. You might be surprised at what you discover. Perhaps you have a hidden talent for painting, or a passion for gardening, or a knack for coding. The possibilities are endless, limited only by our own imagination and willingness to explore.

Here are some practical steps you can take to reignite your passions:

1. Create a Passion Inventory:

Start by making a list of all the activities you enjoyed in the past, no matter how seemingly insignificant they may seem now. This could include hobbies, interests, skills you learned, or even just things you found yourself drawn to. Think about what you enjoyed doing as a child. What were you passionate about before life's responsibilities took over? Consider what brings you joy in the present moment. What are the things you find yourself gravitating towards, even if you don't have much time to pursue them? Reflect on what you've always wanted to try, but haven't had the courage or opportunity to do.

2. Embrace Curiosity:

Be open to exploring new interests and trying new things. Don't be afraid to step outside your comfort zone. Visit a local art gallery, attend a workshop on a new skill, or join a group for people who share your interests. Don't be afraid to experiment and have fun! Remember that passion is a journey, not a destination. There will be times when you're not sure what you're doing, or you feel like you're not good enough. But that's okay. The important thing is to keep exploring and keep learning.

3. Make Time for Your Passions:

Schedule time in your week for activities that bring you joy. Even if it's just for 30 minutes a day, make sure you prioritize your passions. Remember, you are not just a wife, a mother, or an employee. You are also a unique individual with your own interests and desires. Don't let the demands of life crowd out the things that make you feel alive.

4. Find Your Tribe:

Connect with people who share your passions. This can provide inspiration, support, and a sense of community. Join online forums or groups dedicated to your interests, attend local events, or start your own group. Surround yourself with people who encourage your growth and celebrate your achievements.

5. Celebrate Your Progress:

Recognize and acknowledge your accomplishments, no matter how small they may seem. Celebrate your efforts and the progress you're making towards pursuing your passions. Don't be too hard on yourself if you don't always feel like you're moving forward. Every step, no matter how small, is a step in the right direction. Remember that rekindling your passions is a process, not an overnight transformation. It takes time, patience, and a willingness to explore. Don't be afraid to make mistakes, to stumble, to start and stop, and to start again. The most important thing is to keep moving forward, to keep exploring, and to keep nurturing the flames of your passions.

Personal Anecdotes: It's a universal truth that the passage of time can sometimes leave us feeling a bit lost, like we've strayed from the path of our true selves. For me, this realization came during a period of intense career growth. I was juggling the demands of motherhood, a full-time job, and a budding writing career. While outwardly successful, I felt a growing emptiness within. It wasn't until I stumbled upon a forgotten box of childhood treasures – drawings, poems, and old journals – that I began to reconnect with the woman I used to be. There, amidst the relics of my past, lay the dormant embers of my passion for writing. I dusted off my old journal, the faded ink whispering stories from a time when I felt limitless. Each page was a window into my soul, revealing a yearning for creative expression that had never truly left me. That day, I decided to reclaim my passion, to rewrite the narrative of my life. I joined a local writing group, surrounded myself with like-minded individuals who understood the allure of storytelling. I started small, writing for a few minutes each day, then gradually building up to longer sessions. It wasn't always easy. There were days when I felt overwhelmed, frustrated, or like I was simply not good enough. But I persevered, fueled by the rediscovery of a passion that had always been a part of me.

Over time, my writing evolved, my voice grew stronger, and the joy of creating stories filled me with a renewed sense of purpose. I realized that reclaiming my passion wasn't just about writing. It was about reclaiming my identity, my voice, and my sense of self. My journey to reclaim my passions was a reminder that we are never too old, too busy, or too overwhelmed to reignite the flames within. It's a journey of self-discovery, a testament to the enduring power of passion to illuminate our lives with meaning, purpose, and joy.

The Ripple Effect:

The ripple effect of rediscovering our passions extends far beyond our own lives. When we are living authentically, when we are pursuing our passions with joy and purpose, we inspire those around us. Imagine a mother who, after years of dedicating herself to her family, rekindles her passion for painting. Her children, witnessing her dedication and joy, are more likely to embrace their own unique talents and interests. Or consider a woman who, after finding her voice through writing, feels empowered to speak up for what she believes in. Her courage and authenticity inspire others to find their own voice, to break free from societal expectations and embrace their individuality. When we ignite our passions, we create a ripple effect that touches the lives of others. We inspire, uplift, and empower them to embrace their own dreams and aspirations. We become beacons of light, illuminating the paths of those around us.

So, I encourage you to embark on this journey of self-discovery, to explore the depths of your soul and rediscover the passions that make you feel alive. Remember, it's never too late to reclaim your identity, to reignite the flames of your passions, and to create a life that is true to your unique and beautiful self.

Defining Your Goals

It's time to take a deep breath, sit down with a cup of your favorite beverage, and embark on a journey of self-discovery. Imagine a life where you feel genuinely fulfilled, where your daily actions are aligned with your deepest desires, and where you wake up each morning energized and excited about the possibilities that lie ahead. This is the life we're aiming for, and it starts with understanding what truly matters to you. Think of your values as your internal compass, guiding you towards what you cherish and hold dear. They are the principles that shape your decisions, your actions, and ultimately, your entire life. They are the foundations upon which you build your dreams and aspirations. Ask yourself, "What truly matters to me?" It might be a mix of personal values like honesty, kindness, compassion, creativity, or growth. It could also involve broader values like family, community, or making a difference in the world. Don't be afraid to delve deep into your own heart and soul. This is your personal journey, and only you can truly understand the values that ignite your spirit. Once you've identified your values, it's time to explore your passions. What activities ignite a fire within you? What do you find yourself doing with joy and enthusiasm, even if it's just for a short time?

Passions often stem from our innate talents and interests, the things that come naturally to us. Perhaps you've always loved to paint, write, dance, or travel. Maybe you're drawn to helping others, volunteering your time, or advocating for causes that resonate with your values. It's important to remember that passions can evolve over time. Don't limit yourself to the things you enjoyed as a child. Be open to new experiences and explore different avenues. Life is a constant adventure, and embracing new passions can revitalize your spirit and introduce you to incredible opportunities. Now, let's move on to the exciting realm of goal setting. Goals are like road maps, guiding you towards the life you envision. They give you direction, motivation, and a sense of purpose. When your goals are aligned with your values and passions, they become powerful catalysts for personal growth and fulfillment. But it's crucial to set goals that are realistic and achievable. Don't get caught in the trap of aiming for the moon when you can barely reach the ceiling. Break down large, ambitious goals into smaller, manageable steps. This will help you stay motivated and celebrate each accomplishment along the way. For example, if you've always dreamt of starting your own business, don't just say, "I want to open my own store." Instead, break it down into concrete steps: *1. Research and planning:* Develop a solid business plan, research the market, identifying potential customers, and analyzing your competition. *2. Skill development:* Enroll in relevant courses or workshops to acquire necessary skills in marketing, accounting, or business management. *3. Financial planning:* Save for your start-up costs or explore funding options, like small business loans or investments. *4. Networking and connections:* Connect with industry professionals, mentors, and potential investors. *5. Building your* brand: Establish your online presence and develop a compelling brand identity.

By breaking down your goals into smaller steps, you'll feel empowered to act and celebrate progress. Remember, consistency is key. Even small steps taken consistently over time will lead you closer to your ultimate goal. Here are some helpful tips for defining your goals: *1. Be specific and measurable:* Instead of saying, "I want to be healthier," try, "I want to lose 10 pounds and exercise for 30 minutes three times a week." *2. Set realistic deadlines:* Don't set yourself up for failure with unrealistic deadlines. Break down your goals into manageable timeframes. *3. Identify potential obstacles:* Anticipate challenges you might face and develop strategies to overcome them. *4. Celebrate your successes:* Take the time to acknowledge and celebrate your achievements, no matter how small they may seem. This will boost your motivation and keep you moving forward.

As you embark on this journey of self-discovery, remember that it's not about reaching a destination, but about embracing the journey itself. It's about becoming the best version of yourself, embracing your values, pursuing your passions, and setting goals that ignite your spirit. Life is a constant process of growth and evolution. Embrace the changes, learn from your experiences, and never stop exploring your potential. The journey is just as rewarding as the destination, so savor every step along the way.

The Journey of Self Discovery

The journey of self-discovery isn't a destination you reach; it's a lifelong adventure, an ever-evolving exploration of who you are and what you're capable of. It's about embracing the beauty of imperfection and recognizing that your journey is unique, with its own twists and turns. Imagine a grand tapestry, its threads interwoven with a myriad of experiences. Each stitch represents a moment of growth, a lesson learned, a challenge overcome. The tapestry is never finished, for life is an ongoing process of weaving new threads into its intricate design. Embrace the uncertainty, the moments of doubt and confusion. They are the raw materials from which self-discovery emerges. Don't be afraid to question your assumptions, to challenge the beliefs you've held dear. Embrace the opportunity to learn and grow, even if it means letting go of old patterns and shedding limiting beliefs.

Think of yourself as a sculptor, carefully chiseling away at a block of marble to reveal the masterpiece within. Self-discovery is akin to this process: uncovering the true essence of yourself, layer by layer. It may be messy, it may be challenging, but it's through these trials that you shape the person you're meant to be. One of the most liberating aspects of this journey is recognizing that you don't need to have it all figured out. The journey itself is the reward, the constant process of learning and becoming. There will be times when you feel lost, uncertain, or even afraid. Embrace these feelings as an opportunity for growth.

Remember, it's okay to change your mind, to alter your course as you discover new insights about yourself. You are not bound by past decisions or societal expectations. Your journey is your own, and it's yours to shape. Here are some practical ways to embrace the journey of self-discovery: *Embrace Curiosity:* Approach life with a sense of wonder and curiosity. Be open to new experiences, explore different perspectives, and challenge your assumptions. *Seek out New Experiences:* Step outside of your comfort zone and try new things. Take a class, travel to a new destination, engage in a hobby you've always wanted to try. You might discover hidden talents or passions. *Reflect and Journal:* Set aside time for quiet reflection. Journal about your experiences, your thoughts, and your emotions. This practice allows you to gain valuable insights into your inner world. *Practice Self-Compassion:* Be kind to yourself. Accept your imperfections and acknowledge your strengths. Treat yourself with the same compassion and understanding you would extend to a loved one. *Celebrate Milestones:* Acknowledge and celebrate your achievements, no matter how small they may seem. Each step forward, each lesson learned, is a reason to celebrate your progress.

Remember, self-discovery isn't a destination; it's a continuous journey. It's about becoming the best version of yourself, one step at a time. Embrace the process, celebrate the victories, and learn from the setbacks. Your journey is unique, and it's filled with endless possibilities for growth and transformation.

FIND
yourself
AND
be that

CHAPTER 3

Mastering the Art of Self-Care

The Myth of Selfishness

The concept of self-care often gets a bad rap, being labeled as selfish and indulgent. But the truth is, self-care isn't a luxury; it's a necessity. It's not about pampering yourself with fancy spa treatments or indulging in extravagant shopping sprees. It's about tending to your physical, emotional, and mental well-being, ensuring you have the energy and resilience to navigate the demands of life. Imagine a car that's been driven for miles without any maintenance. The engine starts to sputter, the tires wear down, and the overall performance suffers. You wouldn't expect it to run smoothly forever without regular checkups and tune-ups, right? We are the same way. We need to prioritize self-care to keep our bodies, minds, and spirits functioning at their best. When we neglect our own needs, we set ourselves up for burnout, resentment, and ultimately, a decline in our overall quality of life. It's like trying to fill a leaky bucket; we pour in effort and energy, but without taking time to address the underlying leak, we never seem to get ahead.

Think of self-care as a vital investment in your future. It's not about being selfish; it's about being smart. By taking care of yourself, you're better equipped to handle the challenges of life, to show up for the people you love, and to live a more fulfilling and meaningful existence. There's a common misconception that self-care is only for those who have the time and resources for it. This couldn't be further from the truth. Self-care can be as simple as taking a few minutes each day to breathe deeply, listen to calming music, or journal your thoughts and feelings. It can be as elaborate as going for a hike in nature, taking a hot bath, or spending time with loved ones.

The key is to find what works best for you and to make self-care a regular part of your routine. It doesn't have to be complicated or time-consuming; even a few minutes of mindful self-care can make a significant difference in your overall well-being.

Let's explore some real-life examples to illustrate the vital importance of self-care:

The Overwhelmed Mother: Sarah is a single mother of three, juggling a demanding job and a busy household. She constantly feels stressed and exhausted, neglecting her own needs in the process. She skips meals, works late nights, and pushes herself to the limit, believing that her children's needs are paramount. However, this relentless self-sacrifice is taking a toll. Sarah's patience is wearing thin, her sleep is disrupted, and she finds herself feeling increasingly irritable. She's constantly on edge and struggling to keep up with the demands of motherhood. This scenario highlights the importance of self-care for mothers. Sarah needs to prioritize her own needs, even if it means taking a break from her daily routine. She needs to realize that self-care is not a luxury but a necessity for her to be the best mother she can be.

The Burned-Out Professional: Mark is a high-achieving executive who thrives on pressure and success. He puts in long hours at work, constantly pushing himself to achieve more. He believes that hard work and dedication are the keys to success and that self-care is a distraction. He works late nights, skips meals, and sacrifices his personal time to climb the corporate ladder. However, his relentless pursuit of success is taking a toll on his health. Mark starts experiencing headaches, digestive issues, and difficulty sleeping. His relationships suffer, as he becomes increasingly withdrawn and irritable. This scenario illustrates the importance of self-care for professionals. Mark needs to prioritize his health and well-being, even if it means making some adjustments to his demanding work schedule. He needs to realize that self-care is not a weakness but a strength, empowering him to perform at his best and lead a more balanced and fulfilling life.

The Struggling Student: Emily is a college student who juggles a heavy course load, part-time work, and a demanding social life. She's constantly feeling overwhelmed, juggling her responsibilities and trying to meet the expectations of her professors, colleagues, and friends. She often feels like she's not doing enough, struggling to keep up with the demands of her busy schedule. She frequently sacrifices sleep to study, skips meals to save time, and feels guilty for taking time for herself. This scenario highlights the importance of self-care for students. Emily needs to prioritize her mental health and well-being, even if it means taking a break from her demanding schedule. She needs to realize that self-care is essential for her to succeed in her studies, maintain healthy relationships, and overall well-being.

The Importance of Self-Care for Women: Self-care is especially important for women, who often face unique challenges and societal pressures. Women are often expected to be everything to everyone, juggling multiple roles and responsibilities. They are expected to be successful at work, nurturing mothers, supportive wives, and caring daughters all while maintaining a perfect appearance. This constant pressure can lead to burnout, stress, and anxiety. However, self-care can be a powerful tool for women to reclaim their sense of self, prioritize their well-being, and navigate the demands of life with greater ease.

Challenging the "Selfishness" Myth: The misconception that self-care is selfish stems from a societal conditioning that values selflessness and puts the needs of others above our own. We are often told that being a good mother, wife, or friend means putting our own needs aside and focusing on the needs of those around us. This can lead to a sense of guilt and shame when we try to prioritize our own well-being. However, it is important to understand that self-care is not about neglecting our responsibilities. It is about making sure that we have the energy and resources to fulfill those responsibilities in a healthy and sustainable way. Imagine a pilot trying to fly an airplane with depleted fuel. They wouldn't be able to reach their destination safely. The same applies to our lives. We need to refuel ourselves with self-care to ensure that we can show up for the people we love and achieve our goals.

Benefits of Self-Care: Self-care offers numerous benefits, both physical and mental: *Reduced Stress and Anxiety*: Taking time for yourself can help reduce stress and anxiety levels. Whether it's a relaxing walk in nature, a hot bath, or a good book, self-care can help to calm the mind and release tension. *Improved Sleep:* When you prioritize self-care, you're more likely to get enough restful sleep. Self-care activities can promote relaxation and reduce stress, leading to better sleep quality. *Enhanced Mood:* Self-care can boost your mood and increase your sense of well-being. Engaging in activities you enjoy, whether it's spending time with loved ones, pursuing hobbies, or listening to music, can lift your spirits and create a more positive outlook. *Increased Productivity:* Self-care isn't a waste of time; it can make you more productive. When you're well-rested, relaxed, and feeling good about yourself, you're more likely to be focused, motivated, and able to handle challenges effectively. *Strengthened Relationships*: Self-care can strengthen your relationships. When you prioritize your own needs and well-being, you're more likely to be present and engaged in your relationships. You're also less likely to take your frustrations out on others. *Increased Resilience:* Self-care can help you develop resilience, the ability to bounce back from challenges and setbacks. When you're taking care of yourself, you're building a strong foundation for your emotional well-being.

Self-Care is a Choice: Self-care is a conscious choice, a commitment to prioritizing your well-being. It's not about being selfish; it's about being mindful of your needs and taking steps to meet them. It's about recognizing that you're worthy of care and attention. *Making Self-Care a Priority:* Here are some practical tips for making self-care a priority in your life: *1. Schedule Time for Yourself:* Just as you would schedule important appointments, schedule time for self-care activities. This could be a daily morning routine, a weekly afternoon for a hobby, or a monthly spa day. The important thing is to make time for yourself and stick to your schedule. *2. Identify Your Needs:* What are your individual needs? Do you need more sleep, more time for relaxation, or more social connection? Once you identify your needs, you can start to create a self-care routine that meets them. *3. Start Small:* Don't try to do everything at once. Start with small, achievable steps. For example, you could commit to taking a 10-minute walk every day or listening to calming music for 15 minutes before bed. *4. Be Flexible:* Life is unpredictable, and your needs may change from time to time. Be flexible with your self-care routine and adjust it as needed. *5. Be Kind to Yourself:* Self-care is about being kind to yourself, not about being perfect. Don't beat yourself up if you miss a day or two. Just get back on track when you can. Self-care is an investment in your well-being, an act of self-love, and a commitment to living a more fulfilling and meaningful life. Remember, you're worthy of care and attention. Prioritize your needs, and you'll be amazed at the positive impact it can have on your life.

Creating a Personalized Self-Care Routine

Now that you understand the importance of self-care, it's time to create a personalized routine that works for you. It's not about following a rigid schedule or copying what everyone else is doing. It's about finding those activities that truly nourish your body, mind, and spirit. Imagine yourself as a garden, and self-care is the water, sunlight, and nutrients that keep your flowers blooming.

1. Take a Deep Dive into Yourself

The first step is to get to know yourself better. Sit down with a journal and reflect on these questions: What are your unique needs? Are you someone who thrives on structure and routine, or do you need flexibility and spontaneity? Do you find energy in social gatherings or prefer quiet moments of solitude? Do you get energized by movement and physical activity, or do you recharge through creative pursuits like reading or art? What brings you joy? What activities make you feel truly alive? It could be anything - a long walk in nature, spending time with loved ones, reading a good book, listening to music, trying a new recipe, or simply taking a nap. What are your stressors? What drains your energy and brings you down? Identify your biggest challenges, whether it's work deadlines, family obligations, or personal anxieties. What are your time constraints? How much time can you realistically dedicate to self-care each day or week? Be honest with yourself and don't set unrealistic expectations.

2. Experiment and Explore

Once you have a good understanding of your needs and preferences, start experimenting with different self-care activities. Don't be afraid to try something new, even if it seems unusual or outside your comfort zone. Movement and Exercise: Find a form of exercise that you actually enjoy. Maybe it's a brisk walk in the park, a yoga class, dancing in your living room, or a hike in the mountains. The key is to find something that gets your blood flowing and makes you feel good. Mindfulness and Meditation: Even if you've never meditated before, try it! There are many guided meditations available online or through apps. Start with just a few minutes each day and gradually increase the time as you become more comfortable. Creative Expression: Find ways to unleash your creative side. It could be painting, drawing, writing, playing music, cooking, or anything else that sparks your imagination. Social Connections: Spend quality time with people who make you feel good. Schedule regular coffee dates with a friend, join a book club, or volunteer for a cause you care about. Nature and Fresh Air: Get outside and connect with nature. Go for a walk in the woods, sit by a lake, or simply enjoy the sunshine in your backyard. Rest and Relaxation: Give yourself permission to rest and recharge. Take a nap, read a book, listen to calming music, or simply lie down and close your eyes.

3. Tailor Your Routine

As you experiment with different activities, start to build a self-care routine that aligns with your needs and preferences. There is no right or wrong way to do this. Start small: Don't try to do everything at once.

Start with one or two small changes, like taking a 10-minute walk each morning or reading for 15 minutes before bed. Schedule it in: Just like you schedule important appointments, schedule time for self-care. Treat it like a non-negotiable commitment. Be flexible: Life is unpredictable, so be flexible with your routine. If you have a busy day, don't feel guilty about skipping a self-care activity. Just make sure you get back on track as soon as you can. Listen to your body: Pay attention to how you feel after each activity. What makes you feel energized and refreshed? What makes you feel drained or stressed? Adjust your routine accordingly. Don't be afraid to change things up: Your self-care routine should evolve as you do. As your needs and priorities change, so will your self-care practices.

4. Self-Care is Not Selfish

Remember, self-care is not selfish. It's an act of love and kindness towards yourself. When you take care of yourself, you're better able to take care of others. Recharge your battery: Think of self-care as recharging your battery. When your battery is low, you're less able to handle the demands of your daily life. But when your battery is full, you can show up for yourself and others with more energy, focus, and compassion. Invest in your well-being: Think of self-care as an investment in your well-being. It's like putting money in a savings account. The more you invest in yourself, the more you'll have to give to others. Break the cycle of guilt: If you feel guilty about taking time for yourself, challenge those thoughts. You deserve to be happy and healthy. And by taking care of yourself, you're setting a good example for others.

5. Embrace the Process

Creating a self-care routine is a journey, not a destination. It will take time to find what works best for you. Be patient with yourself, celebrate your successes, and don't give up if you slip up. Be kind to yourself: We all have days when we struggle to prioritize self-care. Be kind to yourself and don't beat yourself up if you don't follow your routine perfectly. Just get back on track as soon as you can. Focus on progress, not perfection: It's not about being perfect, it's about making progress. Even small steps towards self-care can have a big impact on your well-being. Enjoy the journey: Self-care should be enjoyable. If you're not enjoying your routine, change it up! Find activities that bring you joy and make you feel good.

Here are some additional tips for creating a personalized self-care routine:

Start with small, achievable goals: Instead of trying to overhaul your entire life, start with one or two small changes that you can realistically maintain. For example, instead of aiming for a 30-minute workout every day, start with 10 minutes, three times a week. Incorporate self-care into your daily routine: Don't just schedule self-care activities for weekends or special occasions. Try to incorporate them into your daily routine. For example, take a 10-minute walk during your lunch break, meditate for 5 minutes before bed, or listen to calming music while getting ready in the morning. Be mindful of your energy levels: Pay attention to when you feel most energized and when you feel most drained. Schedule your most challenging tasks for when you have the most energy and your self-care activities for when you need to recharge. Don't be afraid to experiment: Don't be afraid to try new things. You may be surprised at what you discover. For example, if you've never tried yoga, you might find it's the perfect way to relieve stress and improve your flexibility. Find a self-care buddy: Having someone to support you and hold you accountable can make a big difference. Find a friend who is also committed to self-care and encourage each other to stay on track.

Remember, self-care is not a luxury, it's a necessity. It's about taking care of yourself physically, mentally, and emotionally so you can live a happier, healthier, and more fulfilling life.

The Power of Saying No

The power of saying "no" is not a sign of selfishness; it's a sign of self-respect. It's about understanding your limits, protecting your energy, and prioritizing your well-being. In a world that constantly demands more from us, learning to say "no" is a powerful tool for reclaiming our time and energy and creating space for self-care and personal growth.

Imagine a plate overflowing with food. Each item represents responsibility, a commitment, or a request. It's tempting to try to accommodate everything, to pile on more and more, but eventually, the plate will buckle under weight. That's what happens when we say "yes" to everything without considering the impact on our own well-being. Saying "no" doesn't mean you're being rude or uncaring. It's a healthy way to set boundaries and ensure your needs are met. It's about recognizing that you have a finite amount of time and energy and choosing to invest it wisely in things that truly matter to you.

Here are some practical strategies for setting healthy boundaries and saying "no" with confidence: Identify *Your Values and Priorities:* Before you can say "no," you need to understand what's truly important to you. What are your values? What are your goals? Once you have a clear understanding of your priorities, it becomes easier to say "no" to things that don't align with them. For example, if spending quality time with your family is a priority, you might say "no" to a work project that requires extra hours or a social event that conflicts with family time. *Practice Saying "No" Without Guilt:* Saying "no" can feel uncomfortable, especially if you're used to being people-pleasing. Practice saying "no" in situations where it feels safe and easy. It could be as simple as declining a social invitation you don't feel like attending or saying "no" to a minor request. *Use "I" Statements:* When you decline a request, use "I" statements to express your needs and feelings without blaming or accusing the other person. Instead of saying, "I can't help you with that," try saying, "I'm already overloaded with work right now, and I wouldn't be able to give this my full attention."

Offer Alternatives: If you can't say "yes" to a request, offer alternative solutions. For example, if a friend asks you to babysit their child, but you're already busy, you could suggest other options like recommending a trusted babysitter or offering to watch the child at a different time. *Don't Be Afraid to Say "No" to People You Love:* Setting boundaries with loved ones can be especially challenging. Remember that saying "no" doesn't mean you don't care about them. It means you're prioritizing your own well-being and setting healthy limits. For example, if your mother constantly calls you for advice or asks for help with errands, you might set a boundary by explaining that you need some time for yourself and offer to help in a way that works for you. *Don't Over-Explain Yourself:* You don't owe anyone an elaborate explanation for your decisions. A simple and polite "no, thank you" or "I'm not available at this time" is often enough.

Practice Self-Compassion: Saying "no" can feel like a rejection, even if it's necessary. Practice self-compassion by reminding yourself that you're not obligated to please everyone and that you have the right to prioritize your own needs. *Be Prepared for Pushback:* Not everyone will be happy with your decision to say "no." Be prepared for pushback and resist the temptation to cave in to guilt or pressure. *Use the "Time-Out" Technique:* When you feel overwhelmed by requests, take a moment to step back and breathe. Use this "time-out" to assess the situation and decide what you can realistically handle. *Prioritize Self-Care:* The more you prioritize self-care, the easier it will be to say "no" to things that drain your energy. When you feel refreshed and energized, you'll be better equipped to make healthy decisions for yourself. Setting boundaries and saying "no" takes practice, but it's a valuable skill that can lead to a more fulfilling and balanced life. Remember, you're not responsible for everyone else's happiness. You're responsible for your own well-being, and saying "no" is an act of self-care that empowers you to live a life that is true to your values and priorities. Let's illustrate this concept with a real-life example. Imagine Sarah, a working mother of two, who constantly feels stretched thin. She's juggling a demanding job, household responsibilities, and the demands of her children. Sarah is a people-pleaser and often feels obligated to say "yes" to everyone, even when she's already feeling overwhelmed. One day, Sarah's friend asks her to help organize a fundraiser for their children's school. Sarah knows that she doesn't have the time, but she feels pressured to say "yes" because she wants to be seen as a supportive member of the community. However, Sarah is starting to feel the strain of her commitments. She's constantly tired, stressed, and has little time for herself. She's missing out on spending quality time with her family and her own hobbies. This time, Sarah decides to prioritize her well-being. She takes a deep breath and uses "I" statements to politely decline the request. She explains to her friend that she's currently overwhelmed with her existing commitments and needs to prioritize her time and energy. She offers to help in a smaller way, such as volunteering for a couple of hours on the day of the event. Sarah's friend is initially disappointed, but she understands Sarah's need to set boundaries. She appreciates Sarah's honesty and willingness to help in a way that works for her.

By saying "no" to the fundraising committee, Sarah created space in her schedule for self-care and to spend more quality time with her family. She realized that prioritizing her own well-being wasn't selfish but a necessary act of self-respect. She felt empowered to say "no" to things that didn't align with her priorities and to create a life that was more fulfilling and balanced. Saying "no" isn't always easy, but it's an essential step in reclaiming your time, energy, and well-being. By learning to say "no" with confidence and compassion, you can create the space you need to prioritize your needs and live a life that is true to your values.

Nourishing Your Body and Mind: Imagine a world where your physical and mental well-being are intertwined, where taking care of your body fuels your mind and vice versa. It's not a utopian dream, but a reality you can cultivate through mindful choices. This journey begins with understanding the profound connection between your physical and mental health. Think of your body and mind as two parts of a symphony, each playing a crucial role in creating a harmonious whole. Just like a musician needs to practice and maintain their instrument, you need to nurture both aspects of yourself. This isn't about achieving a perfect physique or becoming a Zen master overnight; it's about making small, sustainable changes that weave into the fabric of your life. Let's start with the physical. Movement, that often-overlooked elixir, holds the key to unlocking energy, improving mood, and boosting cognitive function. It doesn't have to be a grueling gym routine; it could be a brisk walk in nature, a dance class that makes you laugh, or a yoga session that brings tranquility. Find something that you enjoy, something that makes you feel alive, and make it a regular part of your routine. Now, let's talk about food. Think of your body as a garden. What you choose to nourish it with will determine its growth and vibrancy. Instead of resorting to quick fixes and restrictive diets, focus on nourishing your body with whole, unprocessed foods that provide essential nutrients. Imagine a vibrant salad bursting with color, a plate filled with steamed vegetables and lean protein, or a comforting bowl of lentil soup simmered with love. These are not just meals; they are acts of self-care.

And then, there's sleep. A good night's sleep is not a luxury; it's a necessity. It's time for your body and mind to repair and recharge. Imagine your sleep as a deep, rejuvenating bath, washing away stress and fatigue, leaving you refreshed and ready to face the day. Create a relaxing bedtime routine, minimize screen time before bed, and aim for 7-8 hours of quality sleep each night. While physical practice lays the foundation, mental well-being is equally crucial. Think of your mind as a garden that needs tending. It needs to be nurtured with positive thoughts, calming activities, and regular moments of quiet reflection. Start by paying attention to your thoughts. Are they filled with negativity and self-criticism? Or do they radiate kindness and compassion? Just like weeding a garden, cultivating positive thoughts by challenging negative ones.

Meditation, a practice that has been around for centuries, is a powerful tool for nurturing your mental well-being. It's not about emptying your mind, but rather about observing your thoughts and emotions without judgment. Find a quiet space, close your eyes, and focus on your breath. Even a few minutes of meditation each day can create a sense of calm and clarity. Surrounding yourself with nature is another way to nourish your mind. Whether it's a walk in the park, a hike in the woods, or simply gazing out at a beautiful sky, spending time in nature can reduce stress, improve mood, and enhance creativity. The sights, sounds, and smells of nature have a calming effect on the nervous system, offering a welcome respite from the hustle and bustle of everyday life. Connecting with loved ones is essential for mental well-being. Laughter, shared experiences, and genuine conversations are like sunshine for the soul. Make time for meaningful connections, whether it's a phone call with a friend, a dinner date with your partner, or a game night with your family. Human connection is a powerful antidote to loneliness and isolation.

Remember, this isn't about achieving perfection. It's about progress, not perfection. Start with small, sustainable changes that bring you joy and satisfaction. As you nurture your body and mind, you'll discover a newfound sense of energy, focus, and vitality. You'll find yourself more resilient to stress, more capable of achieving your goals, and more deeply connected to your authentic self. Think of it as a journey of self-discovery, a journey that unfolds with each mindful breath, each nutritious meal, each moment of quiet reflection. It's a journey that leads to a more balanced, fulfilling, and empowered life. Embrace the journey, and you'll discover the magic within.

Building a Support System: Imagine a sturdy, comforting oak tree, its branches reaching out, providing shade and shelter to those seeking respite. This tree is a metaphor for the supportive network we all need in our lives, especially as women navigating the complex tapestry of modern life. Building a supportive network is not about simply having a bunch of acquaintances; it's about cultivating meaningful connections with people who genuinely care about you and your well-being. These connections can be with friends, family, or even a therapist, each offering a unique blend of emotional support and accountability. Think of your support system as a diverse and vibrant garden. Each plant, representing a different individual in your life, contributes to the overall health and beauty of the garden. Some plants provide shade and shelter, others bloom with vibrant colors, while others offer a sweet fragrance.

The Power of Friendships: True friendships are like the sturdy, evergreen trees in our metaphorical garden. These relationships provide unwavering support through life's storms, offering a safe space to vent, share joys and sorrows, and celebrate milestones. A good friend listens without judgment, offers a shoulder to cry on, and encourages you to pursue your dreams. Remember Sarah, the single mother struggling to juggle work and raising her two young children? She felt overwhelmed and burnt out. Her friend, Emily, recognized the signs and offered practical help. Emily volunteered to pick up Sarah's children from school a few days a week, giving Sarah precious time to de-stress and recharge. This simple act of kindness made a world of difference, reminding Sarah that she wasn't alone in her struggles.

The Unconditional Love of Family: Family bonds, like the vibrant flowers in our garden, offer a unique kind of support. While friendships often blossom from shared interests and mutual choices, family connections are built on shared history and often, unconditional love. Family members can provide a sense of belonging and acceptance, no matter what life throws your way. Think of Maria, a young woman who had recently moved to a new city for work. Feeling lonely and disconnected, she turned to her sister for support. Her sister, knowing Maria's need for connection, invited her to family gatherings and introduced her to friends, easing her transition into a new environment.

The Professional Guidance of a Therapist: Sometimes, the support we need comes from a professional source, like the gentle, nurturing rain that nourishes our garden. A therapist can provide a safe and confidential space to explore your thoughts and feelings, offering objective insights and guidance to navigate challenging situations. Consider Lisa, a successful businesswoman grappling with anxiety and burnout. She felt like she was constantly on edge, struggling to find a balance between her demanding career and personal life. With the help of a therapist, Lisa learned to manage her anxiety through techniques like mindfulness and deep breathing exercises. Her therapist also helped her set healthy boundaries and prioritize her well-being, leading to a more fulfilling and balanced life.

Building a Supportive Network: Cultivating a supportive network is an ongoing process, one that requires intentionality and effort. Here are some practical tips for building and nurturing your support system: *1.*

Reach Out and Connect: Try to connect with people who you admire, who inspire you, or who share your interests. Don't be afraid to initiate conversations, invite them for coffee, or suggest activities you can do together. 2. *Be Present and Engaged:* When you are with your friends or family, be present in the moment. Listening attentively, offer genuine interest in their lives, and make them feel valued. 3. *Offer Support in Return:* Remember that support is a two-way street. Be there for your loved ones when they need you, just as you would want them to be there for you. 4. *Seek Professional Help When Needed*: There's no shame in seeking professional help when you're struggling. A therapist can provide invaluable insights and tools to navigate difficult situations. 5. *Cultivate Self-Love:* Before you can truly nurture your support network, you need to nurture yourself. Practice self-care, embrace your strengths, and build a strong sense of self-worth. When you feel good about yourself, you're better equipped to offer support to others.

Building a supportive network takes time and effort, but it's worth it. Surround yourself with people who lift you up, encourage you, and celebrate your achievements. These connections will provide a sense of belonging, stability, and empowerment as you navigate the challenges and triumphs of life.

CHAPTER 4

Navigating Relationships with Confidence

Boundaries and Respect

Boundaries are like invisible fences around our hearts and minds, protecting our time, energy, and emotional well-being. They are the lines we draw to define what we are comfortable with and what we are not. In the tapestry of our lives, boundaries are the threads that weave together our values, our beliefs, and our sense of self-worth. Imagine a garden, a space filled with beautiful flowers and vibrant life. It needs careful tending, nurturing, and protection. Without proper boundaries, the garden becomes overrun with weeds, draining its resources and hindering its growth. The same goes for our relationships. Without clear boundaries, we risk being taken advantage of, feeling overwhelmed, and losing sight of our own needs. Setting boundaries is not about being selfish or uncaring; it's about respecting ourselves and our needs, so we can better care for and connect with others. When we have strong boundaries, we can be present and engaged in our relationships, knowing that we are not giving more than we can handle.

The Importance of Boundaries in Relationships: Boundaries are essential in all aspects of our lives, from our personal relationships to our professional ones. They help us maintain healthy relationships, communicate effectively, and avoid feeling drained or resentful. Here's how boundaries play a crucial role: *Protecting Your Time and Energy:* Boundaries help us to say "no" to things that drain our time and energy, allowing us to focus on the things that are truly important. We may say "no" to an extra project at work, a social gathering we'd rather skip, or even a request from a family member that feels overwhelming. *Preventing Resentment:* When we don't set boundaries, we risk feeling resentful of those who take advantage of us. We may start to feel taken for granted, leading to conflict and strain in the relationship. By setting clear boundaries, we ensure that our needs are met, and we can avoid this buildup of resentment. *Enhancing Communication*: Boundaries require clear communication, forcing us to articulate our needs and expectations. This, in turn, helps us to improve our communication skills and learn to express ourselves assertively. It also allows the other person to understand our limits and respect our boundaries.

Setting Boundaries with Your Partner: Relationships, especially romantic ones, can be a beautiful dance of give and take. However, finding a balance between our own needs and those of our partner is essential for a fulfilling and healthy union. *Defining Expectations and Responsibilities:* Open and honest communication about expectations and responsibilities is vital. What are your shared goals for the relationship? How will you divide household chores and childcare? Are there specific needs each of you have that need to be addressed? Having a clear understanding of these aspects prevents misunderstandings and resentment later. *Creating Personal Space:* Maintaining a sense of personal space within a relationship is essential. This doesn't mean you have to live separate lives; rather, it's about respecting each other's time, activities, and interests. This could mean having dedicated time for hobbies, solo pursuits, or simply time alone to unwind and recharge. *Addressing Conflicts and Disagreements:* Disagreements are inevitable in any relationship. It's how we navigate these conflicts that defines the health of the relationship. Setting clear boundaries in these situations means being respectful even when disagreeing, listening to each other's perspectives, and finding solutions that work for both of you.

Navigating Boundaries with Family: Family relationships are often complex and can be challenging to navigate. Family members, because of the inherent closeness, often feel entitled to a certain level of access and influence in our lives. However, it's essential to remember that you have a right to set boundaries with your family members, just as you would with anyone else. *Establishing Distance and Limits:* For some, the idea of setting boundaries with family can feel daunting. However, it's essential to acknowledge that you are entitled to your own space and privacy, even within a family structure. This might involve limiting the frequency of visits, declining requests for help that feel overwhelming, or setting time limits for phone calls or interactions. *Communicating Your Needs Respectfully:* When setting boundaries with family, it's essential to communicate your needs respectfully and firmly. Explain why you need these boundaries and how they benefit your well-being. Be prepared for resistance or defensiveness but stay true to your needs. *Setting Boundaries with Children:* Parenting is a lifelong journey of establishing healthy boundaries. As children grow, their needs and boundaries change. It's important to set clear and consistent boundaries from a young age. This could include bedtime routines, expectations for behavior, and limits on screen time. *Setting Boundaries with Friends:* Friendships are a vital part of our social well-being. However, even in these supportive relationships, it's essential to set clear boundaries to protect your time, energy, and emotional well-being.

Prioritizing Your Needs: Friends can be a source of joy and support. However, it's important to prioritize your needs. You may need to decline invitations to events, politely decline requests for help if you're feeling overwhelmed, or simply take time for yourself to recharge. *Communicating Your Limits:* If a friend consistently pushes your boundaries, it's important to communicate your limits clearly. Let them know what behaviors are acceptable and what are not. It's a good idea to do this in a private conversation, focusing on how their actions affect you. *Evaluating Your Circle:* Occasionally, we may need to re-evaluate our friendships. If a friend consistently disrespects your boundaries, undermines your values, or brings negativity into your life, it may be time to distance yourself from them. *Setting Boundaries at Work*: The workplace can be a demanding environment, where it's easy to get caught up in the hustle and lose sight of our own needs. Setting clear boundaries at work is vital for maintaining a healthy work-life balance and preventing burnout. *Defining Your Work Hours:* Establish clear work hours and stick to them as much as possible. This means limiting overtime, avoiding checking emails after hours, and taking breaks throughout the day. *Protecting Your Time and Energy:* Learn to say "no" to projects or tasks that are not aligned with your role or responsibilities. This can include declining requests for additional work, setting limits on meetings, or even politely refusing to work on weekends or holidays. *Communicating Your Needs:* Be clear with your supervisor about your workload, expectations, and limitations. If you're feeling overwhelmed, don't be afraid to communicate your needs.

Communicating Your Boundaries Effectively: Setting boundaries is only half the battle. The other half is communicating with them effectively. Here are some tips for ensuring your boundaries are understood and respected: *Use "I" Statements:* When communicating your boundaries, use "I" statements to express your feelings and needs. For example, instead of saying "You're always late," say "I feel frustrated when you're late, because it makes me feel like my time isn't valued." *Be Clear and Direct:* Be clear about your expectations and what you are comfortable with. Avoid being passive-aggressive or hinting. *Be Assertive, But Not Aggressive:* Stand your ground, but avoid being aggressive or confrontational. Maintain a respectful and calm demeanor. *Be Prepared to Repeat Yourself:* It may take time for people to adjust to your new boundaries. Don't be afraid to repeat yourself or reiterate your needs. *Be Consistent:* Consistency is key when setting boundaries. If you set a boundary one day and then bend it the next, people will not take you seriously.

The Art of Compromise: While setting boundaries is vital, it's also important to remember that relationships are about compromise. Finding a balance between your needs and the needs of others is key to a healthy and fulfilling relationship. *Be Willing to Negotiate:* Be open to finding solutions that work for both of you. *Focus on Collaboration:* Work together to find ways to meet each other's needs. *Empathize with Others:* Put yourself in the other person's shoes and try to understand their perspective. *Be Flexible:* Be willing to adjust your boundaries occasionally, especially if it's a situation that affects both of you.

Building Strong Relationships through Boundaries: When we set clear boundaries, we communicate our respect for ourselves and for others. This allows us to build stronger, more fulfilling relationships based on mutual respect, trust, and understanding. *Respecting Others' Boundaries:* Just as we expect others to respect our boundaries, we must also respect theirs. Be mindful of the needs of others and avoid pushing or crossing their lines. *Communicating Openly:* Open and honest communication is the cornerstone of any healthy relationship. Be willing to talk about your needs, your expectations, and your feelings. *Building Trust and Empathy:* When we set boundaries and communicate effectively, we build trust and empathy in our relationships. This allows for greater understanding, support, and connection.

The Journey of Boundaries: Setting boundaries is an ongoing process. It requires constant awareness, communication, and a willingness to adjust as our needs and relationships evolve. It's a journey of self-discovery and growth, as we learn to prioritize our well-being without sacrificing our connections with others. *The Power of Saying "No":* Saying "no" can be one of the most powerful acts of self-care. It allows us to protect our time, energy, and emotional well-being. *Saying "No" to Protect Your Time:* If a request or commitment will take away from something that is important to you, it's okay to say "no." *Saying "No" to Protect Your Energy:* If a task or situation will drain your energy, it's okay to decline it. *Saying "No" to Protect Your Emotional Well-being:* If a request or conversation trigger negative emotions or stress, it's okay to say "no."

Conclusion: Setting boundaries is not about isolation or negativity. It's about creating a space for us to thrive, to be present and engaged in our relationships, and to live a life that is true to ourselves. Boundaries are a vital tool for building healthy relationships, maintaining a sense of self-worth, and navigating the complexities of life with confidence. Remember, the journey of setting boundaries is about honoring ourselves, respecting others, and cultivating a life that is filled with genuine connection and authentic happiness.

The Power of Assertive Communication

Assertive communication is a powerful tool that can transform your relationships and empower you to live a more fulfilling life. It's about expressing your needs and feelings clearly and respectfully, without fear of judgment or the need to please everyone. By developing assertive communication skills, you can: *Establish healthy boundaries:* Assertive communication allows you to set limits and communicate your needs clearly, ensuring that your boundaries are respected *Improve communication*: Clear and concise communication leads to better understanding and fewer misunderstandings in relationships *Build stronger connections:* When you communicate assertively, you demonstrate confidence and respect for yourself and others, fostering healthier and more authentic connections *Reduce stress and anxiety:* Assertive communication allows you to express yourself without fear of rejection or judgment, reducing feelings of stress and anxiety associated with holding back your true feelings.

The Pillars of Assertive Communication: Assertive communication rests on three key pillars: 1. *Self-Awareness*: Understanding your own needs, feelings, and values is the first step to communicating them effectively. Ask yourself questions like: What are my needs in this situation? How am I feeling right now? What are my values? 2. *Clear and Direct Expression:* Once you understand your needs and feelings, express them clearly and directly, using "I" statements to take ownership of your thoughts and feelings. For example, instead of saying, "You always make me feel bad," you might say, "I feel hurt when you say that." 3. *Respectful Tone and Body Language:* While asserting your needs, it's important to maintain a respectful tone and body language. Avoid aggression, defensiveness, or a blaming approach. Speak calmly and maintain eye contact, conveying a sense of self-confidence.

Techniques for Assertive Communication: Here are some practical techniques to help you express your needs and feelings confidently: *"I" Statements:* Using "I" statements instead of "You" statements helps to avoid blame and defensiveness. Focus on your own feelings and needs, for example, "I feel frustrated when..." or "I need..." *Active Listening:* Pay close attention to what the other person is saying, both verbally and nonverbally. Reflect back what you hear to ensure understanding and demonstrate empathy. *"Broken Record" Technique:* If someone is trying to interrupt or dismiss your needs, calmly and repeatedly state your point. For example, "I understand your perspective, but I need you to respect my boundaries." *Setting Limits:* Be clear and firm in setting limits on what you are and are not willing to do. Practice saying "no" without feeling guilty or apologetic. *Negotiation:* If a situation requires compromise, approach it with a willingness to negotiate and find mutually agreeable solutions. *Role-Playing:* Practice assertive communication techniques with a friend or family member in a safe and supportive environment.

Common Challenges and How to Overcome Them: Many women find it difficult to communicate assertively, often due to ingrained societal expectations, fears of judgment, or past experiences of being silenced. Here are some common challenges and strategies for overcoming them: *Fear of Rejection:* It's natural to fear rejection, but remember that your needs are valid. Communicating assertively doesn't guarantee a positive response, but it increases the likelihood of your needs being met. *Guilt and People-Pleasing:* You may feel guilty about asserting your needs or prioritizing yourself. Challenge the belief that self-care is selfish. Remember, taking care of yourself is essential to your overall well-being and allows you to better support others. *Fear of Conflict:* Conflict can be uncomfortable, but it doesn't have to be destructive. Approach conversations with a focus on finding solutions, rather than winning or losing. *Past Experiences:* If you have a history of being dismissed or silenced, it may be difficult to speak up. Practice assertive communication in safe spaces with supportive people.

Real-Life Examples of Assertive Communication: Let's look at some real-life scenarios where assertive communication can make a difference:

Scenario 1: Saying No to a Request

Non-Assertive: You feel overwhelmed but agree to take on another task at work because you're afraid to say no.

Assertive: You politely decline the request, explaining that you already have a full workload. You might say, "Thank you for thinking of me, but I'm currently working on a few projects and won't be able to take on anything else at this time."

Scenario 2: Setting Boundaries with Family

Non-Assertive: Your in-laws constantly ask you to babysit, even when it's inconvenient for you. You feel resentful but don't say anything.

Assertive: You set clear boundaries with your in-laws, explaining your limits. You might say, "I love spending time with the kids, but I need more notice to make arrangements. I can only babysit on [days of the week]."

Scenario 3: Expressing Feelings in a Relationship

Non-Assertive: You're feeling neglected in your relationship but avoid discussing it because you're afraid of hurting your partner's feelings.

Assertive: You calmly express your needs and feelings. You might say, "I've been feeling a little neglected lately. I would really appreciate it if we could spend more quality time together."

Conclusion: Developing assertive communication skills is an investment in your well-being and your relationships. It empowers you to express your needs and feelings confidently, leading to greater respect, understanding, and fulfillment. Remember, assertive communication is not about being aggressive or controlling. It's about finding a balance between respecting yourself and respecting others. By embracing these techniques and practicing them in various situations, you can navigate relationships with greater confidence and build a life that feels authentic and fulfilling.

The Art of Compromise

The art of compromise is a delicate dance, a balancing act between honoring your own needs and respecting the needs of others. It's not about sacrificing your well-being to please everyone around you. It's about finding a middle ground where everyone feels heard, understood, and valued. Imagine a tug-of-war, where each end represents your personal needs and the needs of others. Pulling too hard on your side can lead to resentment and frustration, while giving too much ground can leave you feeling depleted and unheard. The key is to find a balanced tension, where both sides are pulling with equal force, creating a sense of harmony and mutual respect. This balancing act begins with honest self-reflection. What are your core needs? What are your non-negotiables? Take the time to understand what truly matters to you. Once you've identified your needs, communicate them clearly and respectfully to others. Don't be afraid to express your desires, but also be prepared to listen to the needs of others.

Remember, compromise is not about surrendering your values or compromising your integrity. It's about finding common ground, exploring creative solutions, and seeking win-win outcomes. Here are some practical strategies for finding a balance between your needs and the needs of others: *Communicate effectively:* Open and honest communication is the foundation of any successful compromise. Clearly express your needs, feelings, and expectations. Be specific and direct, avoiding ambiguity or passive-aggressive language. Listen actively to the perspectives of others, showing empathy and understanding *Be flexible and willing to negotiate:* Approach compromise with an open mind and a willingness to explore different options. Be flexible and adaptable, willing to adjust your expectations if necessary. *Focus on finding mutually beneficial solutions:* Instead of viewing compromise as a zero-sum game, strive for solutions that benefit everyone involved. Look for creative ways to address everyone's concerns and needs. *Prioritize the big picture:* In the heat of the moment, it's easy to get caught up in the details and lose sight of the bigger picture. Step back and consider the long-term implications of your decisions. What's most important in the overall scheme of things? *Set boundaries and maintain your integrity:* Compromise doesn't mean sacrificing your core values or compromising your integrity. Establish clear boundaries, communicating what you're willing and unwilling to compromise on. *Practice empathy and understanding*: Put yourself in the shoes of others, trying to understand their perspective and motivations. Empathy can go a long way in fostering a sense of collaboration and finding common ground. *Be willing to apologize and forgive:* Mistakes are inevitable in any relationship. Be willing to apologize for any hurt or misunderstanding you may have caused. Be willing to forgive others for their mistakes, creating a space for healing and growth.

It's important to note that compromise is not always easy. It requires effort, patience, and a willingness to put aside your ego. But the rewards are immeasurable. By finding a balance between your own needs and the needs of others, you can build stronger, more fulfilling relationships. Here's a real-life example: Imagine you are a working mom who feels constantly pulled in different directions. Your husband wants more quality time together, your children need your attention, and your job demands your focus. You're feeling overwhelmed and stretched thin. Instead of giving in to the pressure and trying to be everything to everyone, you decide to prioritize your needs. You make a list of your core values: family, career, personal growth, and well-being. You communicate with your husband about your feelings, expressing your desire for more support and time for yourself. Together, you come up with a plan where he takes on more responsibility for the children's evening routine, allowing you some time for personal reflection or relaxation. You also schedule regular date nights to reconnect and prioritize your relationship. You find a new way to manage your workload, setting clear boundaries with your colleagues to protect your time and energy. Through honest communication and a willingness to compromise, you find a balance that works for everyone. You're no longer feeling overwhelmed, and you're able to give your best to all the different roles in your life.

The journey of compromise is a continuous process. It's about ongoing communication, adaptability, and a willingness to learn and grow together. It's about building relationships where everyone feels valued, respected, and heard. Remember, the art of compromise is not about giving up your needs, but about finding a way to meet them in a way that honors the needs of others as well. It's about building a tapestry of interconnected lives, where each thread contributes to the beauty and strength of the whole.

Strengthening Relationships

Relationships are the heart and soul of a fulfilling life. They provide us with love, support, companionship, and a sense of belonging. However, relationships can also be a source of stress, conflict, and disappointment. The key to navigating relationships with confidence lies in fostering mutual respect, understanding, and empathy. These qualities are essential for building healthy and fulfilling connections that enrich our lives.

Mutual Respect: Mutual respect is the foundation of any strong relationship. It means valuing and appreciating the other person, even when we disagree with them. Respecting someone's opinions, beliefs, and choices, even if they differ from our own, is crucial. This includes listening attentively to their perspectives, acknowledging their feelings, and refraining from belittling or dismissing their thoughts. When we show respect to others, we create a safe space for open and honest communication, fostering trust and connection.

Understanding: True understanding goes beyond simply hearing someone's words; it involves trying to see the world through their eyes. It means considering their background, experiences, and perspectives, even if they differ from our own. This requires active listening, empathy, and a willingness to put ourselves in their shoes. When we make an effort to understand someone else, we break down barriers and foster genuine connection.

Empathy: Empathy is the ability to understand and share the feelings of another person. It's about stepping outside of our own perspective and experiencing the world from their viewpoint. When we empathize with someone, we show compassion, care, and concern for their well-being. We acknowledge their emotions, validate their experiences, and offer support without judgment. Empathy is a powerful tool for building strong and lasting connections.

Cultivating Mutual Respect, Understanding, and Empathy: Building healthy relationships based on mutual respect, understanding, and empathy requires conscious effort and a commitment to personal growth. Here are some practical tips: *Active Listening:* Engage in active listening, focusing on truly understanding the other person's perspective. Put away distractions, make eye contact, and avoid interrupting. *Empathy Statements:* Use empathy statements to show you understand their feelings. For example, you could say, "It sounds like you're feeling really frustrated right now." *Non-Judgmental Communication:* Approach conversations with an open mind and avoid judgment. Express your opinions and feelings respectfully, even if they differ from the other person's. *Seek Common Ground:* Instead of focusing on differences, look for common ground and shared values. This helps to build a sense of connection and understanding. *Apologize Sincerely:* When you make a mistake, apologize sincerely and take responsibility for your actions. *Be Patient and Understanding:* Remember that relationships take time and effort. Be patient with yourself and the other person as you learn to navigate your differences. *Seek Professional Help:* If you're struggling to communicate effectively or resolve conflicts in your relationships, consider seeking professional help from a therapist or counselor.

The Importance of Empathy: Empathy is often overlooked in relationships, but it is a crucial element in fostering connection and intimacy. When we empathize with someone, we connect with their emotional world and show them that we care about their well-being. This can lead to a deeper understanding of their needs and a more fulfilling relationship. For example, imagine a couple who is experiencing difficulties. If the husband is feeling overwhelmed and stressed about work, his wife can show empathy by acknowledging his feelings and offering support. She could say something like, "I can see that you're feeling really stressed about work. Is there anything I can do to help?" This simple act of empathy can make a significant difference in his emotional state and strengthen their bond.

Strengthening Relationships Through Communication: Communication is the lifeblood of any relationship. It's how we share our thoughts, feelings, and experiences with others. Effective communication is essential for fostering mutual respect, understanding, and empathy. Here are some tips for improving communication in your relationships: *Speak from "I" Statements:* Use "I" statements to express your feelings and needs without blaming or attacking the other person. For example, instead of saying, "You always make me feel bad," you could say, "I feel hurt when you say that." *Active Listening:* Practice active listening by paying attention to what the other person is saying, both verbally and nonverbally. *Choose the Right Time and Place:* Pick a time and place where you can have a calm and focused conversation. *Validate Feelings:* Acknowledge and validate the other person's feelings, even if you don't agree with them. *Seek Compromise:* Be willing to compromise and find solutions that work for both parties. *Take Breaks:* If the conversation becomes heated, take a break and come back to it later when you're both calmer. *Focus on the Positive:* Don't dwell on negative experiences. Instead, focus on the positive aspects of your relationship and express your appreciation for the other person.

The Power of Forgiveness: Forgiveness is a powerful tool for healing and strengthening relationships. When we forgive someone, we let go of resentment and anger, freeing ourselves from the pain of the past. Forgiveness doesn't mean condoning the other person's actions; it means choosing to move forward and create a healthier relationship.

Prioritizing Your Needs in Relationships: While fostering mutual respect, understanding, and empathy is crucial, it's also essential to prioritize your own needs in relationships. You can't truly give to others if you're not taking care of yourself. This means setting healthy boundaries, communicating your needs effectively, and refusing to compromise your well-being.

Setting Boundaries: Boundaries are essential for protecting your time, energy, and emotional well-being. They define what you're willing to do and what you're not willing to do in a relationship. Boundaries can be difficult to establish, especially if you're used to people-pleasing, but they're crucial for creating a healthy and balanced relationship. Here are some tips for setting healthy boundaries: *Identify Your Values:* What is important to you? What are your non-negotiables? *Communicate Clearly:* Express your boundaries directly and assertively. *Enforce Your Boundaries:* Be consistent in enforcing your boundaries. If someone crosses a line, let them know and hold your ground. *Communicating Your Needs:* Once you've set boundaries, it's crucial to communicate your needs clearly and respectfully. This involves expressing your feelings and desires, even if they're difficult to articulate. It also requires being assertive and not being afraid to ask for what you need.

Refusing to Compromise Your Well-being: In any relationship, there will be times when you need to say no. This might involve turning down a request, setting a limit on your time or energy, or prioritizing your own needs. It's important to remember that you have the right to prioritize your well-being and refuse to compromise your values. *Building Healthy Relationships:* Building healthy and fulfilling relationships takes time, effort, and a commitment to personal growth. By cultivating mutual respect, understanding, and empathy, setting healthy boundaries, and communicating your needs effectively, you can create relationships that support, nourish, and enrich your life. Remember that relationships are a two-way street. You need to be willing to give as much as you receive. But most importantly, prioritize your own well-being and refuse to compromise your values. When you do this, you create a foundation for healthy, fulfilling, and meaningful relationships that enrich your life.

Embracing Your Authentic Self

We all have this innate desire to be liked, to be accepted, and to be loved. It's a natural human instinct to crave connection and belonging. But somewhere along the way, for many of us, this desire can morph into something that becomes all-consuming: people-pleasing. People-pleasing is a subtle yet powerful force that can quietly erode our sense of self. It's the constant urge to please everyone around us, even if it means sacrificing our own needs, values, and boundaries. We become so focused on what others think that we lose sight of who we truly are. Imagine a woman named Sarah, a dedicated wife and mother, who always put the needs of her family first. She excelled at baking, planning birthday parties, and volunteering at her children's school. Sarah was the epitome of a "good" wife and mother. However, beneath this facade of perfection, Sarah felt a growing sense of emptiness and dissatisfaction. She had lost touch with her own passions and interests, feeling like a mere shadow of her former self. Sarah's story is not unique. Many women find themselves in similar situations, caught in the relentless cycle of people-pleasing. We convince ourselves that if we just try a little harder, if we just do a little more, we'll finally earn the approval and validation we crave. But the truth is, we are worthy of love and acceptance, not for what we do, but for who we are.

So how do we break free from this cycle of people-pleasing and embrace our authentic selves? It's a journey that requires courage, self-awareness, and a willingness to let go of the need to control outcomes. Here's a roadmap to guide you on your journey towards authenticity:

1. Recognize the People-Pleasing Pattern: The first step in breaking any habit is to become aware of it. Pay attention to your thoughts, feelings, and behaviors. Ask yourself questions like: Do you often feel obligated to say "yes" even when you want to say "no"? Do you prioritize others' needs over your own? Do you find yourself constantly seeking validation and approval from others? Do you feel resentful or exhausted after spending time with certain people? Do you avoid expressing your true feelings for fear of upsetting someone? If you resonate with any of these questions, it's a good indication that people-pleasing might be a pattern in your life.

2. Understand the Roots of People-Pleasing: Once you recognize the pattern, it's important to explore its roots. Why do you feel the need to please others? This could stem from: *Childhood experiences:* Perhaps you grew up in a home where pleasing parents or caregivers was crucial for feeling loved and accepted. Cultural or societal influences: Societal expectations for women to be nurturing, supportive, and always agreeable can perpetuate people-pleasing tendencies. *Fear of rejection*: The fear of disapproval or rejection can drive us to suppress our true selves and conform to others' expectations. *Low self-esteem:* If you don't feel worthy of love and acceptance for who you are, you might be more prone to seeking external validation. Understanding the underlying reasons for your people-pleasing behavior allows you to address them with greater awareness and compassion.

3. Reclaim Your Power: Setting Boundaries: Setting boundaries is a powerful act of self-love and self-respect. It's about defining what's acceptable and unacceptable in your life, what you're willing to tolerate, and what you're not. Boundaries allow you to protect your energy, time, and emotional well-being. Think of boundaries as invisible fences around your life. They are not designed to exclude people, but rather to create a safe and secure space for you to grow and thrive. Here are some tips for setting healthy boundaries: Start small: You don't have to overhaul your entire life overnight. Begin with small steps, like saying "no" to a request that you don't feel comfortable fulfilling. Be assertive: Communicate your boundaries clearly and directly. Use "I" statements to express your needs and feelings without blaming others. For example, instead of saying "You're always asking me for favors," you could say "I feel overwhelmed when I'm asked to do too much." Be consistent: Don't waver or make exceptions to your boundaries unless you genuinely want to. Consistency helps reinforce your limits and prevents others from taking advantage of you. Be prepared for pushback: People may initially resist your boundaries, especially if they're accustomed to getting their way. Stay firm and reiterate your needs calmly. Setting boundaries may feel uncomfortable at first, but it's a necessary step in living a more authentic and fulfilling life.

4. *Embrace Your Authentic Self: Be True to Yourself:* Authenticity is about being true to yourself, regardless of external expectations. It's about embracing your unique qualities, values, and beliefs without fear of judgment. Here's how to embrace your authentic self: Explore your interests: What makes your heart sing? What activities bring you joy and fulfillment? Don't let fear or obligation prevent you from pursuing your passions. Define your values: What's most important to you? What principles guide your decisions? Identifying your values helps you make choices that align with your core beliefs. *Express your thoughts and feelings:* Don't suppress your true feelings for fear of confrontation or rejection. Find healthy ways to express yourself, whether it's through writing, journaling, or talking to a trusted friend. *Surround yourself with supportive people:* Choose to spend time with people who appreciate you for who you are and support your journey towards authenticity. *Practice self-compassion:* Be kind to yourself. Embrace your imperfections and celebrate your progress, even if it's small. Embrace your authentic self with courage and grace. You are worthy of love and acceptance for who you are, not for who you try to be for others.

5. *Letting Go of the Need for Approval:* One of the most liberating things you can do is to let go of the need for external validation. When you constantly seek approval from others, you give away your power. It's like handing over the steering wheel of your life to someone else. Here are some strategies for letting go of the need for approval: *Challenge your beliefs:* Where does the belief that you need approval come from? Is it a deep-seated fear or a learned behavior? Questioning your assumptions can help you break free from limiting beliefs. Focus on your own values: Rather than seeking validation from others, align your actions with your own values. This will lead you to a sense of inner peace and fulfillment. *Practice gratitude:* Shift your attention to the positive aspects of your life. Express gratitude for the people who genuinely care about you and for your own unique strengths. Remember your worth:

You are worthy of love and acceptance, regardless of what others think. This is a profound truth that you must believe in your heart. Letting go of the need for approval is a process, not an overnight transformation. But each time you choose to act in accordance with your own values, you reclaim a piece of your power.

6. Creating a Safe Space for Authenticity: Embracing your authentic self can be daunting, especially if you've spent years trying to please everyone. It's important to create a safe space for yourself to explore your true self without judgment. Here are some ways to create a safe space for authenticity: *Journaling:* Write down your thoughts, feelings, and experiences without censoring yourself. Journaling allows you to process your emotions, explore your values, and discover your true self. *Meditation or mindfulness:* Meditation and mindfulness practices help calm your mind, reduce stress, and connect you with your inner self. *Creative outlets:* Express yourself through art, music, dance, or writing. These creative outlets allow you to tap into your authentic voice and explore your emotions. *Connect with like-minded people:* Surround yourself with people who value authenticity and support your journey. Find a community of women who are on a similar path. *Seek professional help:* If you're struggling to embrace your authentic self, consider seeking guidance from a therapist or counselor. They can provide support and tools to help you navigate this process. Remember, you are not alone on this journey. Many women struggle with the desire to please others, but it's possible to break free and live a life aligned with your true self. Embrace the process, be patient with yourself, and celebrate each step you take towards authenticity. You are worthy, you are capable, and you are deeply loved.

small
STEPS
every
DAY

CHAPTER 5

Embracing Your Self-Worth

The Power of Positive Self-Talk
Imagine a constant inner voice, a chorus of whispers that often paint a less-than-flattering picture of ourselves. It might tell us we're not good enough, not smart enough, or not worthy of happiness. This is the power of negative self-talk, a pervasive inner critic that can chip away at our confidence and self-worth. It's like having a tiny, relentless gremlin perched on our shoulders, constantly spewing doubts and criticisms, undermining our every move. But there's a way to silence that gremlin and cultivate a more positive internal dialogue. This is where the power of positive self-talk comes in, a conscious effort to replace negative thoughts with empowering, self-affirming statements. Think of it as re-placing the gremlin with a wise, encouraging angel, guiding us towards self-belief and resilience. Here's the thing: our thoughts are not facts. They are simply interpretations of our experiences, colored by our past, our beliefs, and our fears. When we become aware of the negativity, we can start to challenge those thoughts and replace them with more con-structive ones. It's like re-framing the story we tell ourselves, rewriting the narrative from one of self-doubt to one of self-belief.

Practical Techniques to Challenge Negative Self-Talk: 1. *Identify the Negative Thoughts:* The first step is to become aware of the negative self-talk. Pay attention to the recurring thoughts and phrases that pop into your mind. You might notice yourself saying things like, "I'm not good enough," "I'll never be successful," or "I'm not smart enough."

Start a journal or a note on your phone to record these thoughts as they arise. This act of noticing is the first step towards changing the pattern. *2. Challenge the Negative Thoughts*: Once you've identified the negative thoughts, it's time to challenge their validity. Ask yourself: - *Is this thought based on facts or feelings?* Is there concrete evidence to support this negative thought, or is it simply an emotional response? - *What would I tell a friend in this situation?* Would you offer them the same harsh judgment you're applying to yourself? - *What is the evidence that contradicts this thought?* Look for examples that challenge the negative thought and support a more positive perspective. *3. Re-frame the Negative Thoughts:* Instead of dwelling on the negative, re-frame the thought into a more constructive and empowering one. For example, if you catch yourself thinking, "I'm not good enough," you can re-frame it to, "I am capable and I am learning and growing." This shift in perspective can help you move forward with a sense of optimism and determination. *4. Embrace Self-Affirmations:* Self-affirmations are positive statements that we repeat to ourselves to reinforce our desired beliefs and values. They work by training our minds to focus on what we want, not what we fear. Some examples of self-affirmations include: - "I am strong and capable." - "I am worthy of love and happiness." - "I am confident and capable of achieving my goals." Repeat these affirmations regularly, especially in moments of doubt or uncertainty. The more you practice, the more they become ingrained in your subconscious mind.

Building a More Positive Internal Dialogue: 1. Practice Gratitude: Focusing on gratitude helps to shift our attention away from negative thoughts and towards the positive aspects of our lives. Take time each day to reflect on what you are grateful for, no matter how small. This practice helps to cultivate a more positive mindset. *2. Celebrate Your Achievements:* Don't underestimate the power of celebrating your accomplishments, both big and small. Acknowledge your efforts and celebrate your progress, even if it's a small step forward. This reinforces your self-belief and motivates you to continue striving towards your goals. *3. Surround Yourself with Positive People:* Our relationships have a significant impact on our self-esteem. Surround yourself with people who up-lift and encourage you, who celebrate your strengths and support your growth. Limit your exposure to negative individuals who drain your energy and foster self-doubt. *4. Engage in Activities That Nourish Your Soul:* Spend time pursuing activities that bring you joy, fulfillment, and a sense of purpose. Whether it's painting, writing, dancing, or spending time in nature, engaging in these activities helps you connect with your authentic self and fosters a sense of well-being. *5. Seek Professional Support:* If you find yourself struggling with negative self-talk and feel unable to overcome it on your own, don't hesitate to seek professional help. A therapist can provide guidance and strategies to help you challenge negative thought patterns and develop a more positive and empowering self-image.

Examples of Positive Self-Talk in Action: Imagine a woman named Sarah who is a stay-at-home mom. She constantly feels overwhelmed by the demands of motherhood and household chores. She often catches herself thinking, "I'm a terrible mom, I'm not doing enough, and I'm not even a good cook." Sarah can use the techniques mentioned above to challenge these negative thoughts: 1. Identify the Negative Thoughts: She recognizes her recurring thought: "I'm a terrible mom." *2. Challenge the Negative Thought:* She asks herself: "Is this based on facts or feelings?" She realizes it's based on feelings of inadequacy and pressure. *3. Reframe the Negative Thought:* She replaces the negative thought with "I'm doing my best, and I'm learning and growing as a mom." *4. Embrace Self-Affirmations:* She starts saying affirmations like "I am a loving and nurturing mom" and "I am capable of providing a loving and supportive home for my family." As Sarah continues to practice these techniques, she gradually shifts her inner dialogue from one of self-criticism to one of self-acceptance and self-compassion.

The Power of Transformation: The journey of challenging negative self-talk and cultivating positive self-talk is a continuous process, a life-long practice of self-discovery and self-love. It's not about eliminating negativity altogether, but rather about learning to recognize and manage it effectively. It's about finding a balance between self-awareness and self-compassion, acknowledging our limitations while celebrating our strengths. By embracing this power, you can unlock the potential within, building the confidence, resilience, and strong sense of self that you deserve. Remember, you are worthy, you are capable, and you are deserving of happiness and fulfillment. Start with a simple shift in your internal dialogue, and watch as your life transforms for the better.

Cultivating Gratitude

Gratitude, often referred to as the "attitude of grace," is a powerful force in cultivating a sense of contentment and self-worth. It is a conscious shift in focus, directing our attention towards the positive aspects of life, rather than dwelling on what we lack or what might be going wrong. By practicing gratitude, we cultivate an appreciation for the small, everyday joys and acknowledge our achievements, big or small. Imagine a woman named Sarah, a mother of two young children and a full-time employee, feeling overwhelmed with the constant demands of her life. She often finds herself frustrated, comparing her life to others who seem to have it all – picture-perfect families, successful careers, and endless free time. This constant comparison fuels a sense of inadequacy, leaving her feeling depleted and unfulfilled. One day, while driving home from work, Sarah noticed a breathtaking sunset, its vibrant hues painting the sky in a kaleidoscope of colors. She paused for a moment, mesmerized by its beauty, and a wave of appreciation washed over her. In that moment, she realized that amidst the chaos of her life, there were still moments of beauty and joy, moments worth appreciating. This experience sparked a shift in Sarah's perspective. Inspired by this newfound awareness, Sarah decided to cultivate gratitude in her daily life. She started by writing down three things she was grateful for each evening before going to bed. At first, it was a challenge to find something positive in the midst of her hectic schedule, but gradually, she began to notice the small things that brought her joy: a heartfelt hug from her children, a shared laugh with her husband, a moment of quiet reflection during her lunch break. Sarah also made a conscious effort to acknowledge her accomplishments. She started a gratitude journal, where she documented her achievements, no matter how small they seemed. From completing a work project on time to successfully navigating a challenging parenting situation, she celebrated her successes, big and small. This practice boosted her confidence, reminding her of her capabilities and helping her to see herself in a more positive light.

Cultivating gratitude is a journey, not a destination. It requires conscious effort and practice, but the rewards are immeasurable. It shifts our focus from what we lack to what we have, fostering a sense of contentment and appreciation. Here are some practical strategies for cultivating gratitude in your own life:

1. Start a Gratitude Journal: Set aside a few minutes each day to write down three things you are grateful for. This could be anything from a warm cup of coffee in the morning to a successful meeting at work. *Be specific.* Instead of simply writing "I'm grateful for my family," try writing, "I'm grateful for the laughter my children bring to my life." Include both big and small things. Don't overlook the simple joys that often go unnoticed. Review your journal regularly. Reading through your past entries can remind you of all the good things in your life and reinforce your sense of gratitude.

2. Practice Gratitude Meditations: Guided gratitude meditations can be a powerful tool for deepening your appreciation. There are many guided meditations available online or through meditation apps. Focus on your breath and bring to mind things you are grateful for. It can be a simple act of gratitude for the ability to breathe or the feeling of warmth in your body. Start with a few minutes each day and gradually increase the time as you feel comfortable.

3. Create a Gratitude Jar: Write down things you are grateful for on slips of paper. These can be short phrases, words, or even drawings. Place the slips of paper in a jar. Whenever you are feeling overwhelmed or down, take a few moments to read through the entries in your gratitude jar. It can be a powerful reminder of all the good things in your life.

4. Express Gratitude to Others: Take the time to thank people for their kindness, support, or help. This can be a simple "thank you" or a heartfelt letter. Perform acts of kindness for others. This could be anything from helping a neighbor with their groceries to volunteering at a local charity. Expressing gratitude to others not only strengthens your relationships but also cultivates a sense of positivity and connection. 5. Incorporate Gratitude into Your Daily Routine: Start your day by reflecting on things you are grateful for. This could be a simple act of appreciation for a good night's sleep or a healthy breakfast. End your day by expressing gratitude for the people and experiences in your life. This can be a powerful way to end the day on a positive note. Find opportunities to express gratitude throughout the day. It can be a simple "thank you" to a cashier or a smile to a stranger.

6. Embrace Mindfulness: Mindfulness is the practice of paying attention to the present moment without judgment. It involves being fully aware of your thoughts, feelings, and sensations, without getting caught up in them. Cultivating mindfulness can help you to appreciate the simple moments in your life. It can help you to notice the beauty and wonder in everyday experiences, from the scent of your morning coffee to the warmth of the sun on your skin.

7. Challenge Negative Thoughts: It's natural to have negative thoughts from time to time. When these thoughts arise, try to challenge them. Ask yourself, "Is this thought really true? What evidence do I have to support this thought?" Replace negative thoughts with positive affirmations.

8. Celebrate Your Achievements: Don't be afraid to celebrate your accomplishments, no matter how small they seem. This could be anything from finishing a work project to completing a workout or learning a new skill. Take the time to acknowledge your efforts and recognize your progress. Rewarding yourself for your achievements can boost your confidence and motivate you to continue striving for your goals.

9. Focus on the Present Moment: Dwelling on the past or worrying about the future can prevent you from appreciating the present moment.

Try to focus on what you are doing right now. Engage all your senses and appreciate the beauty and wonder of the present moment.

10. Be Patient with Yourself: Cultivating gratitude is a journey, not a destination. It takes time and practice to develop a consistent sense of appreciation. Be patient with yourself and don't be discouraged if you don't see results immediately. Celebrate your progress, no matter how small it may seem. The journey of cultivating gratitude is a powerful path to self-worth. It empowers us to shift our focus from what we lack to what we have, fostering a sense of contentment and appreciation for the everyday joys and our personal achievements. This practice can transform our lives, leading to a more fulfilling, meaningful, and joyful existence.

Resilience and Growth

Life, especially for women, can feel like a relentless marathon, with countless hurdles and unexpected detours along the way. We juggle demanding careers, nurturing families, maintaining households, and managing social commitments, often feeling overwhelmed and drained. It's easy to succumb to the pressure, questioning our worth and wondering if we're doing enough. But amidst the chaos, it's crucial to remember that resilience is not just a quality we possess; it's a muscle we can strengthen. Every challenge, every setback, is an opportunity for growth. Instead of viewing obstacles as insurmountable barriers, let's reframe our perspective and embrace them as stepping stones on our journey toward self-discovery and fulfillment. We can learn from every experience, even the most challenging ones, extracting valuable lessons and emerging stronger on the other side. Think of a tree that has weathered countless storms. Its sturdy roots, hardened by years of adversity, allow it to withstand the fiercest winds. Its branches, scarred and twisted, tell stories of resilience and adaptation. Similarly, our life experiences, even those that feel painful and difficult, shape us into resilient individuals, capable of navigating life's complexities with grace and strength.

Let's consider the concept of resilience in the context of motherhood. Becoming a mother is a transformative experience, filled with overwhelming joy, immense love, and countless challenges. Sleepless nights, endless demands, and the constant pressure to be the "perfect" mother can take a toll on our physical and emotional well-being. Yet, within these challenges lies an incredible opportunity for growth. Motherhood teaches us about patience, selflessness, and the profound strength we possess. It pushes us to our limits, forcing us to dig deep and tap into reserves of energy we didn't know we had. Each obstacle we overcome, each hurdle we clear, strengthens our resilience, making us more capable of handling future challenges. Think of a young mother struggling to balance her demanding career with her new role as a parent. She may experience feelings of guilt, inadequacy, and exhaustion. But as she navigates these complexities, she learns to prioritize, delegate, and ask for help when needed. She discovers a level of resourcefulness she never knew she had, learning to adapt and thrive in a constantly changing environment. This is a testament to the power of resilience. By embracing challenges as opportunities for growth, she becomes a stronger, more capable woman, not only for herself but also for her child. The same principle applies to our relationships, both personal and professional. Conflicts, misunderstandings, and even heartbreak can be viewed as opportunities for learning and growth. They force us to examine our communication styles, our boundaries, and our ability to forgive. By embracing these challenges and seeking solutions, we build emotional intelligence, deepen our understanding of ourselves and others, and foster more meaningful and fulfilling relationships.

Think of a woman who has experienced a difficult break-up. Initially, the pain and heartbreak may feel overwhelming. But as she processes her emotions and learns from the experience, she discovers a newfound strength and self-awareness. She learns to prioritize her well-being, set healthier boundaries, and develop a stronger sense of self-worth. This journey of resilience can be a powerful catalyst for personal transformation. Here are some practical strategies to embrace resilience and transform challenges into opportunities: *Cultivate a growth mindset:* Instead of viewing setbacks as failures, embrace them as opportunities for learning and improvement. Remember that every challenge presents a chance to grow and develop new skills. *Practice self-compassion:* Be kind to yourself during difficult times. Acknowledge your feelings without judgment and offer yourself the same understanding and support you would give to a friend. *Seek support:* Don't be afraid to reach out to trusted friends, family members, or professionals for support. Sharing your burdens with others can lighten the load and offer valuable perspectives. *Develop coping mechanisms:* Identify healthy ways to manage stress and navigate difficult emotions. This may include exercise, meditation, journaling, spending time in nature, or pursuing hobbies. *Focus on the positive:* Make an effort to acknowledge the good things in your life, even during challenging times. Gratitude can shift your perspective and remind you of your strength and resilience. *Celebrate your progress:* Acknowledge your achievements, both big and small. Recognizing your accomplishments, even in the face of adversity, can boost your confidence and reinforce your resilience.

Remember, resilience is not about being immune to challenges; it's about our ability to navigate them with strength, grace, and determination. By embracing a growth mindset and viewing setbacks as opportunities for learning, we can emerge from adversity stronger, wiser, and more capable than ever before. Let's not shy away from life's challenges, but instead, embrace them as opportunities for growth and transformation. Each hurdle we overcome makes us more resilient, more capable, and more prepared to navigate whatever life throws our way. Embrace your inner strength, cultivate a growth mindset, and remember that within every challenge lies the potential for incredible personal growth.

Celebrating Your Strengths

Imagine a treasure chest overflowing with precious jewels, each one representing a unique talent, skill, or strength you possess. These are your gifts, the qualities that make you special, the things you do exceptionally well, and the abilities that set you apart. But how often do you pause to truly appreciate these gems? How often do you acknowledge and celebrate the amazing person you are? Many of us are so focused on what we lack or what we need to improve that we overlook the incredible strengths we already possess. We get caught up in comparing ourselves to others, diminishing our own unique value. It's time to break free from this limiting mindset and start appreciating the amazing person you are. Think about your strengths as a superpower. Each one is a unique and valuable ability that can help you achieve great things. Whether it's your creative flair, your problem-solving skills, your ability to connect with people, or your unwavering determination, these strengths are a source of power and confidence.

Here are a few steps to help you uncover and celebrate your strengths:

1. Reflect on your past successes: Start by taking a journey through your memories. Reflect on moments when you felt proud, accomplished, or truly in your element. What did you do that led to these positive outcomes? What skills did you use? What qualities did you draw upon? Think about projects you successfully completed, challenges you overcame, or situations where you excelled. What did you learn from these experiences? What did they reveal about your strengths? For example, did you demonstrate exceptional organizational skills in planning a successful family event? Did you show great resilience in overcoming a personal setback? Did you use your creativity to come up with an innovative solution to a problem?

2. Ask for feedback from trusted people: Sometimes it's hard to see our own strengths. We are too close to the situation to notice our positive qualities. That's why seeking feedback from trusted individuals can be invaluable. Ask your partner, friends, family members, or colleagues to share their observations about your strengths. Ask them questions like: What are some of my best qualities? What am I good at? What strengths do I bring to the table? Their perspectives can shed light on areas where you shine and offer insights you might have missed. Remember, genuine feedback from people who care about you can be a powerful tool for self-discovery.

3. Engage in activities that highlight your strengths: Think about activities that naturally bring you joy and fulfillment. What are you drawn to? What tasks do you find easy and enjoyable? By engaging in these activities, you naturally highlight and nurture your strengths. For example, if you enjoy public speaking, volunteering to give presentations at work or joining a public speaking group will help you hone your communication skills and boost your confidence. If you are a natural problem solver, taking on challenges at work or volunteering to help others find solutions to their problems will allow you to utilize this valuable strength.

4. Acknowledge your strengths regularly: Make a conscious effort to acknowledge your strengths on a regular basis. Create a list of your strengths and keep it in a visible place where you can see it daily. Read it aloud and remind yourself of your amazing qualities. When faced with a challenge, remember your strengths and how they can help you navigate the situation. For example, if you are feeling overwhelmed by a demanding task, remind yourself of your organizational skills and how they can help you prioritize and manage your workload. This simple act of self-affirmation can boost your confidence and empower you to tackle challenges with grace and resilience.

5. Use your strengths to help others: One of the most fulfilling ways to celebrate your strengths is by using them to help others. When you share your gifts and talents with the world, you make a difference and create a positive impact. This can be as simple as offering advice to a friend, mentoring a colleague, or volunteering your time to a cause you care about. By using your strengths to make a difference in the lives of others, you not only elevate them, but you also experience a sense of deep fulfillment and personal satisfaction.

6. Embrace your unique journey: Remember that everyone is unique, and your journey is a testament to your individuality. Don't compare yourself to others. Focus on your own strengths, your own passions, and your own goals. Embrace the fact that you are one of a kind. Celebrate your unique gifts and talents. They are a source of strength, confidence, and joy. As you acknowledge and appreciate the amazing person you are, you unlock a powerful sense of self-worth that empowers you to live a fulfilling and authentic life.

The Journey Continues

As you stand at this juncture, having navigated the chapters that have led you to this point, remember that this isn't the end of your journey—it's a new beginning. You've unearthed your values, rediscovered your passions, and established a foundation for self-care. You've honed your communication skills, set healthy boundaries, and embraced the power of positive self-talk. You've learned to celebrate your strengths and find joy in the everyday. But the most crucial element of this transformative journey is the unwavering commitment to self-love, acceptance, and continuous growth.

Self-love isn't a destination; it's an ongoing practice. It's about treating yourself with the same kindness, compassion, and understanding you'd offer a beloved friend. It's about recognizing your worthiness, celebrating your achievements, and forgiving yourself for your imperfections. It's about acknowledging your emotions, both positive and negative, without judgment or suppression. Self-love isn't about being narcissistic or arrogant; it's about cultivating a deep and abiding respect for the incredible being you are.

Acceptance is another essential pillar of this journey. It's about embracing who you are, flaws and all. It's about recognizing that you're not perfect, that you'll make mistakes, and that you'll encounter challenges along the way. It's about accepting that you are enough, just as you are. Acceptance doesn't mean resigning yourself to mediocrity. It's about recognizing your strengths and weaknesses and embracing them as part of your unique tapestry. Continuous growth is the heartbeat of this journey. It's about constantly learning, evolving, and expanding your horizons. It's about challenging yourself to step outside your comfort zone, embrace new experiences, and pursue your passions with unwavering determination. It's about never settling for the status quo, always seeking new ways to improve, and striving to become the best version of yourself. The beauty of this journey is that it never truly ends. There will be ups and downs, triumphs and setbacks, moments of clarity and periods of doubt. But amidst the ebb and flow of life, remember the fundamental principles that have guided you this far. Continue to nurture your self-worth, practice self-love and acceptance, and embrace continuous growth. This is the key to unlocking a life of fulfillment, purpose, and lasting happiness.

As you embark on this ongoing journey of self-discovery, remember that you're not alone. There are countless women who have walked this path before you, each with their unique story and challenges. Connect with other women who share your aspirations and challenges, seek out mentors and support systems, and draw strength from the collective wisdom of those who have come before you. This isn't just about achieving a perfect life; it's about embracing the imperfections. It's about finding joy in the simple things, celebrating the small victories, and learning from every experience. It's about living a life that resonates with your values, nourishes your soul, and inspires you to grow.

So, let your journey continue. Let your self-worth shine brighter each day. Let your self-love be your compass, guiding you through the twists and turns of life. Let your acceptance be your anchor, keeping you grounded amidst the storms. And let your growth be your engine, propelling you forward with purpose and passion. For within you lies the power to create a life that is truly your own. The life you were meant to live. The life that reflects your unique brilliance and embodies your unwavering self-worth.

Acknowledgements

This book would not exist without the unwavering support of my incredible family and friends. Thank you to my husband, Lee for your love, encouragement, and unwavering belief in me. To my children, Kaylee, Elizabeth and Fisher; your laughter, hugs, and unconditional love are my greatest inspiration.

A special thank you to my dear friend, Diana, for your insightful feedback, honest perspectives, and unwavering support throughout this journey. Your encouragement and belief in my work have been invaluable.

And to all the women who have shared their stories and experiences with me, thank you for your vulnerability and for inspiring me to write this book. Your strength and resilience are a testament to the power of finding your self-worth.

Courtney resides in Georgetown, South Carolina with her husband and two children. Working on obtaining a law degree, Courtney put her love for writing on the back burner until recently, when she unexpectedly lost her brother. This change prompted Courtney to pursue her writing path again, and here she is writing books from the heart, she hopes to encourage everyone to follow their dreams, no matter how big or small.

Courtney spends most of her time crafting, reading, and snuggling up with her three dogs when she is not writing.